For my daughter Johanna Stickland

FROM THE CORNER OF **BAD AND ASS**

ILLUSTRATION: CARRIE SCHIFFLER

FROM THE
CORNER OF

BAD
AND
ASS

CARRIE
SCHIFFLER

DURVILE &
UpRoute Books

Calgary, Alberta, Canada

Durvile & UpRoute Books

DURVILE IMPRINT OF DURVILE PUBLICATIONS LTD.

Calgary, Alberta, Canada
DURVILE.COM

LIBRARY AND ARCHIVES CATALOGUING IN PUBLICATIONS DATA

From the Corner of Bad and Ass: True Stories
Schiffler, Carrie, author

MEMOIR

Durvile Reflections Series. Series editor, Lorene Shyba.

978-1-988824-81-9 (pbk)
978-1-990735-00-4 (ebook)
978-1-990735-01-1 (audiobook)

Book design, Lorene Shyba
Front cover photograph, Loretta Meyer
Back cover photograph, Johanna Stickland

Durvile Publications would like to acknowledge the financial support of
the Government of Canada through Canadian Heritage Canada Book Fund
and the Government of Alberta, Alberta Media Fund.

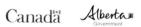

Printed in Canada. First edition, first printing. 2022.

This book is memoir. It reflects the author's present recollections of experiences over time.
Some names have been changed and some dialogue has been recreated. The statements,
views, and opinions contained in this book are solely those of the author. Neither the
publisher nor the editors are responsible for accuracy.

PRELUDE

H E LOOKED at my copy of The Glass Castle I had placed on the hospital bedside table. Sneering openly, he asked, "What do you think of the book?" I gave Nurse Don a non-committal, "It's okay."

It was prize-winning memoir. I was a quarter of the way through. I've been reading autobiographies and memoirs since I was a kid, beginning with The Diary of Anne Frank. True life accounts of enduring hardships and overcoming injustices gave me hope that I too could win at life despite the shitty hand I was dealt. Now as a fifty-whatever-year-old writer of my own memoir, I read them to see what my competition is.

While Nurse Don fiddled with the intravenous bag, I asked, "I take it you're not a fan?"

"I'm sorry, but anyone who says they remember what happened to them when they were like three years old, I mean come on. She's gotta be making that stuff up. It's like that guy, that drug addict who's book won a ton of awards. He was even on Oprah. They found out most of it was a lie and now he's got a movie deal!"

"A Million Little Pieces," I offer

"Right! The book with all the donut sprinkles on the cover."

I wanted to correct him and tell him those aren't donut sprinkles—they are pills, multicoloured drugs. He's a nurse. Shouldn't he know that?

I stayed quiet. Why argue with the person preparing me for a colonoscopy.

This exchange with Nurse Don, brought a brief wave of self-doubt. What if after dredging up the past, sifting through the sludge and then painstakingly assembling the muck into a readable form, no one believes me?

Well, it wouldn't be the first time I was accused of lying, and it won't be the last. I learned a long time ago that while it may be my duty to be truthful, I have zero control over how my truth is received. So some may say these stories are too outrageous or too tragic to be true. I say, what better reasons are there to not share them?

1

BEGIN TO REMEMBER
THE BEGINNING

MY EARLIEST MEMORY is of being baptized. How is that possible? I was still a mewling baby, yet clear as yesterday I remember being held by a strange man with foul breath. He rambled on while dripping water on my head. I cried and flailed, looking around the room for something comforting. My eyes found Oma. My dad's mom. She was standing up in the front row, a sturdy 4′10″ pillar of German practicality, stuffed into a boxy, two-piece tweed number and dabbing sanctimonious tears with a white handkerchief. Oh, how I loved everything about her: the goofy accent, her perfume of lye soap and mothballs, and most importantly her unconditional love of me. This baptism was all her idea. She believed that should a person die before being baptized they were doomed to spend eternity frying in the flames of Hell. My parents believed that a baptism meant presents, preferably presents in the form of cash. Lorraine, my mom, was 20 and Anton, my dad, was 21. Between the two of them they had a grade 9 education. Dad worked odd jobs while Mom stayed home with me and my half-sister, Tracey. Tracey was a year older than me and who her father was, was anyone's guess. Before you get all judgy, this was the sixties, the age of opening your mind, heart, and legs to love and drugs.

Even though the sperm source was a mystery, it was no mystery to Lorraine that her own parents wanted nothing to do with an illegitimate grandchild. With no familial or financial support, Lorraine's baby was made ward of the Crown and placed in foster care. Some time later, Mom met Dad and together they convinced the Powers That Be they were ready to provide a stable home for Tracey. Mom was reunited with her firstborn. The happy couple married and I was conceived on their honeymoon which was spent at the Burk's Falls Hotel in room 6.

I don't know when the abuse started. The details dribbled down to me over the years, coming in drunken fits and starts. The following is what I heard more than once from both Mom and Dad.

I WAS 3, TRACEY 4. Dad came home from work to an empty house. He panicked and made a bunch of phone calls. We were finally tracked down at Ruth's place. Ruth was a friend of my mom's. She lived two blocks away in the Ontario housing complex on the other side of the street. Mom had taken us there because she had hurt Tracey and was afraid of Dad finding out. Rightfully so. He too was a hothead, prone to violent outbursts. When he caught up with us and saw the bruises on Tracey he punished his wife by beating the shit out of her. The police came. My dad was hauled off to jail. My mom had a nervous breakdown and was taken to the Queen Street Mental Institution. My sister and I were sent to a foster home.

While I have zero memory of that tragic day (thank God), I have some very clear recollections of our new temporary placement. The mother figure had a mousy nest of hair and worried eyes. She was sweet most of the time but her tactics to get me to eat healthy were circumspect. She'd often say, "If you want to see your mom again you'd better eat all your peas." To

Lorraine and Tracey, my mom and sister.
They did not have much time together before she was
handed over to another family.

this day just the smell of peas makes me gag. I also remember a teenage girl who grabbed me by the shoulders and shook me until I felt my brain clang against my skull.

I remember a visit to a special doctor too. I was excited. I had never been to a special doctor before. I was told this special doctor would help decide when I could go home again. I missed Mom so bad. I couldn't mess this up. He made me draw pictures of my family. Easy. I loved drawing! I was also shown a series of coloured blobs and was supposed to say what they looked like. One looked like blood on the kitchen floor but a little voice inside told me that 'butterfly' was a better answer. I passed with flying colours. Tracey didn't do as well.

I remember Tracey vividly. She was larger than life. She had a mass of curls on top of a long skinny body, round blue eyes and a wide smile. Her energy was boundless. While I was often sick and listless, she was always on the move, like a caffeinated monkey. I tried my best to keep up. When she told me there was finger paint in the bathroom, I was right there beside her smearing toothpaste and shaving cream on the walls. She convinced me we had to cut the pillows "cuz the feathers wanted to fly again." When she wore her bowl of Alphagetti's as a hat, I had to follow suit. I could not say no to her. She was full of brilliant ideas and it's not like we had a ton of toys to keep us occupied. Although, we did have a Fisher-Price record player. Man, we loved that thing. We fought over it all the time.

I don't remember how much time we spent in the foster home.

I do remember being taken to the Queen Street Mental Institution to visit Mom. A grownup held my hand through the echoey hallways to the cafeteria where Mom was waiting. She sat at a large table, dressed in a pale starchy gown that was more animated than her face. I wanted to run to her, jump into her lap and give her the biggest hug ever. I was held back and reminded she was still very sick, too sick for any excitement. I obeyed and gave her a gentle kiss on the cheek instead. Her eyes did not meet mine. I sat across the table from her and stared. While the grownups talked at her I willed her to get better, to smile, to look at me, just look at me.

I remember a care package from Oma. She sent chocolate and crochet slippers. She was denied temporary custody. There was no one to help her with the paperwork. All

Looking a little worse for wear, Tracey and Carrie
perch on the brown couch at the corner of Bad and Ass.

---

she could do was cry and plead her case in broken English.
My Uncle Ralph was furious and wanted to take care of us too.
He was only 17.

I remember the day the big white car came to take Tracey
away. She was going to be given a fresh start with a new family.

There was no sunshine. Everyone was as sad as the day was
grey. I was instructed to say goodbye to my sister. We hugged.
I cried. I might never see her again. I didn't want to let her go.
The grownups pulled us apart. I picked up the Fisher-Price
record player and gave it to her for good. I got to be raised by
our birth mom. Tracey got the consolation prize. Or did she?

During her stint in hospital Mom was diagnosed with partial schizophrenia. Partial schizophrenia? How is that even possible? Is that the same as being somewhat pregnant? Would that diagnosis even jive today? She was dosed with several rounds of electric shock treatments.

I remember the day I left the foster home. A small blue car driven by a friendly social worker, Mrs. Cornflower, pulled up. I kid you not. Cornflower was her name. Mom liked to talk about this day. She referred to it as, 'the day me and Mrs. Cornflower got you back.' There were a lot of tears. Happy tears. Even the mousy-haired foster mom cried. She gave me a doll too. I played with it in the back seat. Mom sniffled away upfront while Mrs. Cornflower comforted her in hushed tones.

Home smells like Pine-Sol and stale cigarettes. Next door a coin drops and rolls across the floor. A neighbour sneezes. We're at the dining room table. Mom sits with legs crossed, shoulders rounded forward. One arm protects her belly, the other is propped up on the table holding a cigarette. She stares at me. Her mouth smiles but there's fear in her eyes.

MOM: Would you like a drink, sweetie?
ME: Yes, please.
She gets up, readying herself for Mom Mode. This time she's going to do it right.
I gulp down the water and ask for more. She brings me another. I drink it down even faster and show her my empty cup.
ME: More please.
MOM: You're a thirsty girl!

Carrie and Tracey thriving in foster care.

I had more cups of water, one right after the other. It's not that I was actually thirsty as much as I was amazed. Here was my very own mom taking care of me. I asked for water, and she would get up and go to the kitchen. Better yet, she returned each time with the plastic orange cup of water. She could have been empty-handed, I didn't care. She came back. That's all that mattered. She came back for me.

2

TAKE IT TO THE BRIDGE

I HAD TO WEAR MY PURPLE SNOWSUIT. It was too small. Every time I lifted my arms it felt like I was going to split in half. I knew better than to complain. Mom had just yelled at the cats for staring at her. She was having wardrobe issues of her own. A button popped off of her long brown coat. She tore through the house, ripping open drawers and slamming them shut before returning with a safety pin.

ME: Can I do that, Mommy?
She hands me the pin and leaned over.
My hands aren't shaky like hers. I get it on the first try.
Me: Now you'll be snug as a bug."
She grunts, opens the door and swears at the cold.

The cold didn't bother me. I loved walking to Safeway. We got to cross a huge bridge that went over eight lanes of highway. I'd wave to all the trucks and do the yanking sign with my hand and they would honk so loud we could feel it in our boots. Sometimes Mom would do the yanking sign with her hand too. I swear they honked even louder for her. I could tell Mom was in no mood for honking today so I kept my hands to myself and thought of Cousin Tammy's Barbie collection.

When we got to the electronic doors of Safeway, I skipped inside to grab a cart. Everything was warm and bright. Mom caught up, grabbed the cart and said, "Don't touch anything."

She steered us through the canned goods with one hand

while the other reached up, across, down and back so fast I could barely see what she was grabbing. She didn't slow down until we approached the fresh fruits and vegetables. It smelled like spring and everything was shiny with water drops. She stopped the cart in front of a mountain of the biggest reddest apples I'd ever seen. We stared and I wanted one so bad but I stayed quiet. Apples were not on the grocery list she had written on the back of her cigarette pack.

Mom didn't say a word until we left the store and she swore at the cold again.

The walk home is never as fun as the walk somewhere else.

I didn't look for big trucks.

We had our heads down, toques against the wind.

There was no way we could have missed them. In the middle of the bridge, right there on the sidewalk, at our feet, sat a red apple and a golden pear glowing in the slush!

We look at each other, look at the ground, and look at each other again. Mom picks up the fruits, turn them in her hands and says, "We'll give them a good wash first," before gently placing them in one of the grocery bags. The rest of the walk flies by. We grew Tigger feet and bounce all the way home.

To this day, we can only guess how the miracle fruit came to be.

Did someone see us in the produce aisle and take pity?

Or maybe someone's bag broke and two perfectly delicious pieces of fruit rolled out and just happened to land in the middle of our path.

Were we being watched or watched over?

3

MOURNING DEVOTIONS

THE KIDS IN MY NEIGHBOURHOOD were tough. Playdates would inevitably end with me getting hurt in some way. Kimmy Kable was queen of the bullies. She'd knock on my door all smiles asking if I could come out and play. If Mom needed a break from my relentless whining about how bored I was she'd let me go but not without first advising me, "Fight back and slap that shit-eating grin off her face."

I never fought back. Even when Kimmie Kable made Leanna Whorl pin my arms behind me so she could stick butts in my mouth and yell, "Inhale bitch!" I did nothing. It was like my fight or flight switch was broken. It must have been fiddled with too many times. Fine. I needed friends to play with. This bitch inhaled.

Thankfully the Kables moved away before I became a pack-a-day smoker. I returned to the solitary activities of an only child: reading, colouring, and watching television. I wished the Brady Bunch would adopt me. It would be so fun to have brothers and sisters. Gilligan's Island was another favourite. I was going to be just like Ginger when I grew up.

My lonely world changed when the Middels moved in down the hall. This family of six were all clean, freckled, bespectacled, and extremely religious. They were like a Dutch-Canadian version of the Waltons. They did not fit into our neighborhood at all. Even better than that, they had a girl my age! Geraldine was quick to become my best friend and I was keen to tag along to all their family outings. This meant going to church twice on Sundays, bible study on Tuesdays, and Pathfinders (Girl Guides for Christ) on Fridays. I became a bible-toting, scripture-quoting Born Again Christian, much to Mom's chagrin.

One night after a particularly rousing worship session I went home to find Mom listening to Pink Floyd. Fuelled up on self-righteousness, I stormed over to the stereo, lifted the needle off the record and said, "I can't have this devil's music playing in my house." I was sent to my room. The music was turned up. I prayed for Mom. I prayed for myself. Being a Born Again Christian was a tough gig for a welfare kid. I was surrounded by heathens. It was best I spend as much time with the Middels as possible.

Of course I could go to summer camp with the 'Jesus freaks.' Mom didn't even pause to flick her ash when I showed her the pamphlet. Promising a 'safe haven for underprivileged kids, Kamp Kuriou will guide your precious gift closer to God with daily crafts, boating, and campfire fun! Nestled in the cedar woods of northern Ontario, your child will be embraced by the love of Christ in every sunrise, and soothed to sleep by the loon's sweet lullaby.'

We got the subsidy and the sleeping bag. Mom dutifully wrote my name on all my personal effects and off I went to spend two weeks in the woods with my bestie!

ON THE SURFACE, Kamp Kuriou looked like any other summer camp. Boys' cabins on one side, girls' cabins on the other. Between the two sat the mess hall. There was also a gym, boat dock, and tuck shop. Nothing fancy, but compared to the corner of Bad and Ass, this was a slice of heaven on Earth. I got to sleep in a bunk bed and hang with Geraldine, every day. The best part was, I got a break from the drunken drama at home.

Because Kamp Kuriou was all about saving the poor little poor kids, we had to do a shit ton of praying. We had morning devotions at 6 a.m. where everyone gathered in silent prayer on the hill overlooking the lake. I didn't mind this. It was pretty at that time of the day and I preferred praying in my head, quietly to myself. The other devotion sessions were noisy. We were expected to throw our hands up and shout unto the Lord. Apparently, if your neighbours can't hear you, neither can God. I didn't want anyone but God to hear me so I mumble-whispered.

My prayers went something like this: "Dear God, could you please send me a boyfriend, a Christian boyfriend who is funny and has long eyelashes. Don't worry. We won't kiss or anything. And dear Jesus, could you keep my dad safe. I miss him so much and I pray Mom is wrong and he's not lying in the gutter somewhere. Amen."

Eventually all that praying paid off. I met a boy. Better yet, I met a boy who liked me! His name was Robert. He corrected anyone who tried to call him Rob, Bob, Robbie, or Bobbie. My name is Robert, thank you very much. What a gentleman. Oh, and his eyelashes were long and thick, framing two dark chocolate-covered almonds for eyes! Robert was perfect. Of course I said yes when he asked if I wanted to go on the moonlit walk with him. This was a group event led by Pastor Bowen and his wife. All of the counsellors and campers would partner up and follow behind our leaders as they guided us through the woods and around the lake. Usually Geraldine and I did the walk together. She was a little sad but very understanding when I told her an actual boy had asked me.

The stars and the moon seemed extra bright that night. It felt like we were under a spotlight, which made me even more nervous. I was sweating in all the wrong places. Up until that point I had never even held a boy's hand. I was 12. So was Robert. He was just as awkward as me. We talked about how much we hated school. I made a mental note to pray for God to forgive me for lying. In front of us and behind us other couples were arm in arm. I desperately wanted to know what that felt like but was too terrified to make the first move. As if reading my mind, Robert came in closer, the hair on our arms touched. I thought I was going to pass out. Just before things escalated to full-blown hand holding, Pastor Bowen appeared beside us. "Hey you two! Enjoying Our Saviour's beautiful light show tonight?"

We both stared up at his doughy face. I forget how to swallow.

PASTOR: Did you know each constellation is made of individual stars that belong to one another? God made it so. Just like people. God made it so that all the white people belong in one constellation and all the black people belong in their own constellation. The two shall never mix.

I wanted to yell at him, "God loves everyone equally. He's not a racist like you." I wanted to fight back, but I didn't. I couldn't. I was stuck on pause cuz it was all my fault. Pastor Bowen knew I wanted Robert to touch me. I looked to the sky, searching for God's forgiveness but saw nothing.

All of the stars were a blur.

That's what happens when you cry.

4

THE SMILE

I'VE ALWAYS LOVED TO SING and would force my cousin Tammy to watch as I sang "Hopelessly Devoted To You" into the extendable arm of the Hoover Upright. I sang a lot of Christian music with the Middels too. Geraldine, her three brothers and I, stuffed into the backseat, would sing all the way to church and all the way back home from church. My favourites were the upbeat tunes. Even "This Little Light of Mine" could be given a jazzy flair.

> *Monday gave me the gift of love*
> *Tuesday peace came from above*
> *Wednesday gave me a little more faith*
> *Thursday gave me a little more grace*
> *Friday told me just to watch and pray*
> *Saturday told me just what to say*
> *Sunday gave me the power divine*
> *Just to let my little light shine*

Whoo!

And then the chorus.

I slipped easily into rock gospel land while the boys gravitated to sweet barbershop harmonies. We'd just be getting into it when Mrs. M, who I both adored and feared, would turn to stare us down. The straight bangs of her bowl cut lay still as she waved her long slim index finger back and forth like a metronome. We had gone too far. Our unbridled version suggested the content was second fiddle to the style.

The song had become more about the singing and less about the Lord. We needed to exercise control lest the 'little light' become a raging fire of passion. She preferred for us to stick to less embellished devotional hymns. Too bad. We could totally rock out to "Go Tell It On The Mountain," which we practiced when she was not in ear shot.

When I was ten I actually got a gift that I'd asked for! It was brand new too. It was a tape recorder, the size of a shoe box, all silver and black with sturdy rectangular buttons. I was dying to hear myself sing. I wanted to know if I sounded as good on tape as I thought I sounded live. Geraldine came over. We stuck our heads together and poured our hearts into the tiny microphone on the bottom-right corner. Never has there been recorded a more sincere version of "500 Miles" or a more emotive rendition of "Both Sides Now." With eyes full of stars we rewound and pushed 'play'. Barely breathing we sat motionless and listened. How could that be? How was it possible that my voice could be both whiny and flat at the same time? This tape recorder must be faulty! To make matters worse, Geraldine sang sweet-n-clear, just like the God-fearing angel she was.

Even though it was obvious I was not the next Olivia Newton John, I didn't let go of my dreams of stardom. It was 1981, also know as The International Year of the Child.

Our grade 4 teacher, Mrs. Smith, tells us about a singer-songwriter competition where young musicians are encouraged to enter a song that captures the spirit of 'The Child.' The winner receives $100 and the chance to perform their song on live television. This could be my big break! Now that I have a tape recorder, the music world was my oyster! How hard can it be to write a song? It's just a poem set to music. I can write a poem. I can't write music but maybe Geraldine can help. She plays the piano. Her whole family takes lessons. They even owned a piano, which some folk thought suspicious, considering she too lived at the corner of Bad and Ass.

After school we ran back to her place. Writing the words was easy, the music part not so much. I could hear the tune in my head clearly. I sang it over and over and over again. Geraldine just could not play it on the piano. She didn't know what chord or key or measure or tempo I wanted. I didn't even know what any of those things meant. Frustrated and impatient, I left in a huff with a head full of award-winning song. Once back home, in the solitude of my bedroom, I successfully recorded an acapella version.

I called the piece "The Smile." It was about being happy because you're a child and how children should show they're happy by smiling. I was deep like that. There was no story arc or a clever use of metaphor but that didn't stop me from bringing my tape recorder to school and sharing my contest entry with Mrs. Smith and my peers.

The room was silent. I pressed 'play'. Out poured my voice. I sounded like a kid trying to sound like an adult. It was godawful. Someone started with a not-so-subtle snicker which soon led to a room full of wheezing side-splitting belly laughs. I slunk behind my desk. The only thing that song had going for it was its length. It came in under 45 seconds. We were all relieved when "The Smile" was no more.

Mrs. Smith tried to come to my rescue, "How dare you laugh! It's very difficult to create music. Carrie was the only one in the entire school to accept the challenge. She should be commended for her efforts."

What was I thinking? The song sucked. I knew it, yet I still willingly pressed play and committed social suicide.

I wish I could say I learned some good lessons that day, like how to trust that internal voice that says, "Don't do it." Nope. Forty years later I still second guess myself, flip the bird to common sense, and throw myself into the deep end like a drunk who can't swim, wildly thrashing about, sputtering, gasping, and then finally surrendering only to discover I didn't die.

Damn.

5

THE GIFT THAT
KEEPS ON GIVING

CHRIST THE KING ANGLICAN CHURCH assembled and distributed Christmas hampers to those in need. Those like us. Mom and I were delighted to find a parcel on our doorstep on December 24. We dragged it inside and politely removed the card taped to the outside of the box. It instructed us to open the parcel immediately as the perishables would need to be refrigerated. The box contained all the fixings for a turkey dinner as well as a couple of nicely wrapped gifts for both of us. I lightly touched the pretty tag, "Merry Christmas, Carey!" Oops, they spelled my name wrong. I would be sure to correct them when I wrote the thank you note! I fondled it, shook it, smelled it and tried to see through the pretty paper. Could it be a Barbie Dune Buggy?! It was the right size.

Mom said, "What are you waiting for, Christmas? Open the damn thing!"

I did as I was told. I opened the damn thing!

Once all the paper was removed there was a moment of silence. I turned it in all directions, checked it out from every angle. Could it actually be? The words on the box confirmed it. For boys 7+. At least they got the age right. The hideous contraption was trademark Tonka, yellow and black. It reminded me of a monster bee from a stupid science fiction show.

Some 7-year-old girls might squeal with delight at receiving a front-end loader. Some 7-year-old girls may have wrongly assigned genitals. Some 7-year-old girls might self-identify as 7-year-old boys. I was not one of them. I self-identified as Barbie and wished to be Barbie when I grew up, with the perfect body, fancy wardrobe and both Ken and Evil Knievel as boyfriends.

There was no hiding my disappointment. I cried. I cried like the little girl I was.

Mom tried to comfort me. "At least now we have something to give to Jeffery. You can give it to him yourself. We're going over there soon."

Jeffery was her then boyfriend's son. We hadn't met yet, but I was told we were the same age. Surely he would appreciate a truck more than me.

And he did! Jeffery played with the truck for hours while I did a paint-by-numbers of a buck in the woods. Later on we were put to bed in the basement guest room. The lights were barely turned off before Jeffery was on me to play husband and wife. I had only played that game with girls before. I said no and spent most of the night kicking at him to stay on his side of the bed. At one point he talked me into checking out the snack situation in the storage room. There wasn't anything edible in there except for a large jar of eggnog crystals. "Just add milk, stir and drink."

Jeffery grabbed a handful, stuffed his mouth and said," "Tateth jut ike candy." Sold. I grabbed the jar from his grubby hands and poured the crunchy goodness straight in. He was right. It tasted just like candy! He told me to shut up. He didn't want to get caught. This stuff was supposed to be for grownups only. We passed the jar back and forth like a couple of hobos hiding in a train car. We polished it off in minutes and then waddled back to bed.

Some time later Jeffery's violent projectile vomiting woke up the whole house. The parental units came flying down the stairs and took in the neon yellow mess all over the bedroom walls. I looked around me with morbid fascination. The volume, the coverage was impressive. Then I saw it, a pool of puke floating in the loader of the Tonka truck. Maybe it was the lack of sleep, maybe it was the sugar, or maybe some part of my brain registered this as absurd retribution, but I started to laugh. It began with a giggle and quickly escalated to full-on wheezy hyena shrieking. I laughed like only a goofy 7-year-old can laugh. Mom looked at me like I was losing my mind. I pointed at the truck. She started to giggle too, quietly at first. Then her shoulders began bouncing up and down and she let out a full-on snort. We were sitting side by side on the edge of the bed. She grabbed my hand and we fell backwards, laughing until we could barely breathe. Best Christmas gift ever.

6

SCHADENFREUDE

AFTER WORK ON FRIDAYS, Dad would drink beer. Sometimes he would drink too much and not come home. Sometimes he would drink a lot and show up late bearing guilt gifts. In German this is known as drachenfutter, gifts given to placate someone, usually a spouse, who is angry at the giver. The literal translation is "dragon food." In our home the dragon food was often alive. Both my parents were animal lovers. However their attitude towards pets differed dramatically. Mom was practical to the point of pessimism, whereas my dad was optimistic to the point of delusional. When a goldfish we had for only two days leapt clear out of its bowl, Mom said, "Goldie committed suicide because even a dumbass fish knows this life is shit." Dad on the other hand took in an abandoned baby raccoon, set up a litter box and bought it a leash for imagined strolls along the beach. Olio, the raccoon, had other plans. His idea of a good time was to flip ashtrays, rip apart the bean bag chair, and help himself to the contents of the fridge.

I was with my dad when he released Olio back into the wilds of Barrie, Ontario. We both cried while Dad reassured me Olio was better off in the forest with lots of other shit-heads he could party with. Over the years my dad staggered through the door with a menagerie of wild things. There was even a spider monkey for a short time. Only one picture remains of Heinz. In it, he is cowering in the corner of our dim basement, terrified and tragic.

There was a series of bunny rabbits too. Of them, my favourite was Bear, the French Lop. He met his demise after eating his way through a garbage bag full of homegrown. We found him in bed lying on his back, clutching a bowl of Cheez Doodles.

Only one drachenfutter enjoyed reasonable longevity and that was a dog. She was a puppy when Dad found her crying at the door of the Cabbagetown Boxing Club. Aside from one black eye, her wiry coat was a yellowed-white as if stained by nicotine. She looked like a cross between a Jack Russell, a Pomeranian, and a meth addict. Mom's first reaction was, "What the hell is it?" I fell in love. Even though Mom thought it was "the ugliest dog ever made," she let me keep it but insisted she name it. That's how Brandy, my childhood dog, came to be.

In 1976 we entered Brandy in the Toronto Star's "Mutt of the Year" competition. Some five hundred Ontarioian mutts barked, sniffed, and humped their way through this all-day affair on the grounds of the then-undeveloped Harbourfront. Brandy was 2 in dog years, which translates to 14 in people years. She was at the height of her geekdom. There were several categories in which one could enter their mutt: Biggest; Smallest; Best Dressed; Most-Looks-Like-Owner; Most Beautiful; and Most Unusual. We figured we had that last one in the bag. Mom also entered Brandy in the Best Dressed category. Brandy was done up like a boxer with blue sateen shorts and a red cape that Mom embroidered ROCKY onto. This was a big deal. Mom hated sewing. If something couldn't be fixed with a glue gun it was tossed. I was proud of her attempt at costume design, until we got to the grounds of the contest that is. Everywhere we looked

Heinz, our pet monkey. The stuff of nightmares.
If my dad had his way, all our pets would
be named after his German relatives.

we were bedazzled with tutus, tiaras, butterfly wings, devil horns, cowboy boots—and that was just the owners. Their dogs were dressed to the nines in outfits no one in my family could ever dream of affording. But the movie Rocky had just been released that year. It was a huge hit. Brandy had a black eye and one of the judges had a sense of irony. That's how our three-pound mongrel became one of the five finalists for Best Dressed! People loved her. As soon as she was brought on stage, the laughter was overwhelming. Poor dear peed right through her sateen shorts. Her bladder was the same size as her brain, according to Mom.

Brandy didn't place for Best Dressed but not surprisingly she won first place for 'Most Unusual Mutt of the Year!' We were given a trophy, a ribbon, and a year's supply of kibble. The coolest prize though was opening the Toronto Star the next day and seeing our winning mutt in all her quivering Dr. Seuss-like glory. We were famous, sort of.

The following year we entered again, confident we had this contest locked down. Brandy was 21. Lucky for us she had not outgrown her awkward phase and, in fact, was even weirder looking. The kibble she won was freely poured and she freely ate. Brandy had developed a paunch. Everything except her belly was still spindle thin, making her look like a thrift store footstool. We didn't bother with the Best Dressed category. We were fully committed to Brandy's incumbency: She would take the Most Unusual Mutt prize for the second year in a row. Oddly, Mom too had gained weight over the past year. She didn't argue when I insisted on being the one to usher Brandy into the Winner's Circle. "I don't want those goddamn cameras snapping in my fat face." The time had come. I had replayed this moment in my head for the last 364 days. Me on stage with Brandy by my side, the winner is announced. We take a step forward. The crowd goes wild. I'm handed a trophy and smile straight into the lens. Click, click, boom!

This is our big day. As predicted, Brandy is a finalist. I slowly parade her across the stage, savouring the enthusiastic round of applause and laughter. The next dog to roll past is Bootsy. She is small with a patchy coat and a face only a mother could love. Bootsy also has a wheel strapped to her back end. Bootsy's unusual characteristic is that she only has two legs.

Me, Geraldine and Brandy.

When the winner was announced, I felt the full impact of the failure of the world to live up to my expectations. The German word for this is weltschmerz. I was frozen on stage with my peeing pet and I started crying like only a disappointed disenfranchised 9-year-old girl can cry. On the drive home my parents offered words of comfort. "Brandy was still the ugliest mutt there. I don't care what anyone says. We'll always have her trophy. No one can take that away from us." I stopped crying at some point that evening and felt fine by the next morning.

Then I went to school.

The entire class was crowded around the Current Affairs corkboard. I pushed my way through the laughing crowd and

SURE IT'S SAD to lose, but there's always next year!

Thanks to this capture in the newspaper,
I was not voted Miss Popularity that year at school.

---

saw what they were mocking. It was me, just me, or rather a black and white photo of me clipped from the newspaper. In it, I'm weltschmerzing all over the place. The caption read, "We know it's sad to lose, but there's always next year." There was no picture of Brandy. I had really hoped they were laughing at my dog. I tried to explain I was crying because I felt sorry for Bootsy. She had a wheel where her back legs should be! That only made them laugh louder, which made me cry harder. My nickname was Crybaby for quite some time afterwards, which inevitably triggered successive crying jags. I leaned heavily on the sticks-n-stones mantra to move on, or as the Germans would say, "Vergangenheitsbewältigung"—get over it!

7

MY GONG-SHOW CRUSH

I'VE ALWAYS HAD a soft spot for the oddballs. Ever since grade school I befriended the weirdos. The quirkier the better.

Sean Reubens wore three-piece suits, cologne, and carried his homework in a briefcase.

Even as an 8-year-old, he was committed to dressing for the job he wished he had. Sean believed he was destined to become a businessman or a stand-up comic. I found his ambition intoxicating! Or maybe it was the Paco Rabanne.

Of course I said yes when he asked me to do a skit with him for Show-n-Tell.

He wanted to do a re-enactment of the Gong Show. Chuck Barris was his idol so, of course, he had to play him. I offered to be a baton-twirling contestant. And then for the grand finale, Sean would stick a paper bag over his head and be the Unknown Comic.

I practiced my baton twirling for a week and choreographed a routine to "Rock Me Gently." My baton skills were very ... limited. I mean, I could throw the rubber-ended piece of metal up to the sky and I could even catch it 50 per cent of the time. I knew I sucked but I didn't care. All that mattered was the leotard. Specifically, Sean Reubens seeing me in that leotard. It was a short-sleeved, navy blue number I wore over black pantyhose. I brought the whole ensemble together with a red kerchief tied around my neck. Sean Reubens was sure to take one look and fall passionately in love. (How could he not?!) I had never been so excited for Show-n-Tell before. I even convinced my mom to take a photo of me on the big day. "Jeezus, Care. You better be wearing some pants on top of that getup."

Our little Gong Show skit was well... a gong show.

Sean opened with a comedic monologue of obscure knock-knock jokes that no one laughed at. By the time I took to the stage, our classmates were already bored. Undeterred, I committed fully to twirling, spinning, and up up up it went! My leotard that is. I was having a growth spurt on the spot. Experiencing my first public camel toe did not stop me from merging with the music. In fact, it helped.

Touching you so warm and tender
Lord, I feel such a sweet surrender
Beautiful is the dream that makes you mine
Mmm
Rock me gently
Rock me slowly
Take it easy
Don't you know
That I have never been loved like this before

I snuck a glance at Mrs. Kowaleski. Her usual valium smile had slid off her face. At that moment she saw my future and it definitely involved a brass pole. She was mortified.

I was spared dancing the entire three and a half minutes of "Rock Me Gently," thanks to Sean. He'd lifted the needle off of the record, threw a paper bag on his head and came staggering to the front of the class, flailing his arms and shouting, "I am the Unknown Comic. I am funny. You should laugh at

All gussied-up for the Gong Show.

me!" The class shouted, GONG! GONG! GONG! Mrs. K snapped back to life and got the audience to calm down long enough for us to take a bow and curtsy, respectively.

That's what a performance high feels like?!?! Sign me up! My little baton routine kick-started a lifelong love of dancing in skimpy costumes.

Later that same year, restless with spring fever and unrequited love, I snuck up on Sean while he was hunched over his desk. It was during Art. He was so focused on his painting he didn't sense my approach. I slipped my hands on either side of his rib cage and squeezed. His head jerked back and then slammed forward right into his desk. He yelped and flew his hands up to his now-bleeding mouth. Mrs. Kowaleski quickly ushered him out of the room, leaving the rest of the grade 3 kids in shocked silence. I was the first to exhale and let out a loud ugly sob. Some of the kids tried to comfort me. "Stop crying, Carrie. Sean will be okay." I knew he was going to be okay. It's not like I killed him. I was crying because I blew my chance. How could he possibly fall in love with me after this?

Sean Reubens returned the next day and I nervously apologized. His new tooth looked great! He would have to get it bonded every couple of years. Instead of being angry at me he made jokes about having his smile rearranged by 'some girl.' I wish I could say that was the last time I hurt him but a few months later a similar accident occurred. We were running back into the school from recess. Sean was behind me and in a grand gesture I swung open the heavy door with a flourish to allow him entrance. We both miscalculated and the metal door hit him right in the honker. Once again there was blood, tears, and a hearty dose of self-loathing. And once again, he forgave me. In fact, a year later he passed me a note in class.

"Dear Carrie, do you want to go around with me?"

Are you kidding me? After all the pain I had caused him he still wanted to be my boyfriend?!

I wrote back, in my most impressive cursive, "Dear Sean. Yes. Thank You, Carrie."

This was the first time an actual boy had actually asked me to go around with him.

That day after supper, we met at the swing set beside Christ The King Church. This was the same church I was baptized in and where I went to Brownies and later on Girl Guides. (Side bar: I was kicked out of Girl Guides for passing around a copy of Judy Blume's Forever. It was considered too adult for us pre-teens. I tried feigning ignorance but the Guide Leader flipped open the book and showed me all the dirty bits I had highlighted in bright yellow. Busted.)

We sat swinging side by side and talked about Gilligan's Island and how we hoped they would just get rescued already. And how Kazoo ruined the Flintstones and wouldn't it be fun to take a cruise on the Love Boat someday.

We tried to swing over the bar and got so high the entire swing set thumped off the ground.

Then we played spin-out. We twisted our swings in one direction as far as we could, then lifted our feet letting the chains unwind, spinning wildly in the opposite direction. Our seats clanged together and for a moment the hairs on our arms touched. Dizzy and giddy, we both ran home in opposite directions.

The next day another note made its way to my desk.

"Dear Carrie. I'd like to take you to see Kramer vs Kramer and then for Swiss Chalet on Saturday. Sincerely, Sean"

"Dear Sean. This is moving too fast for me. Sorry. I can't go around with you anymore. Sincerely, Carrie"

I was not ready for an actual date-date. We were only ten for crying out loud.

There was no way my mom would let me go to a movie theatre with a boy.

I felt bad enough for lying to her the day before.

I had told her I was going to the swing set with Dini instead of Sean.

And what would God think?

This backsliding into temptation had to stop before it got worse and I became a full-on Jezebel.

Sean did not take rejection well. He pouted while his guy friends glared at me on the playground.

Eventually Sean forgave me. Some forty years later he agreed to meet for a catch-up.

We met in Yorkville at a swanky Gastro Pub. It was an unusually warm September. TIFF was in town and everyone was dressed to impress, including Sean Reubens. He wore a tan-coloured sports jacket with matching pants and a white mock turtleneck. His hair looked glued in place. It was still a dusty blond with a deep side part. The only startling change was his skin. There were lumps and bumps on his face which he had tried in vain to cover with a strong-smelling foundation. I wanted to ask about his skin but he already seemed self-conscious enough. We shared the highlight reels of the past decades. After graduating from seminary school, he was a minister for a spell until the original dream of being a comic pulled him out of the pulpit and into the unforgiving stand-up scene.

He hinted at some mental health struggles and attributed them to his reason for residing in his mom's basement.

We laughed about our turbulent past and he showed me the slight discoloration of his bonded tooth.

Neither of us ever did see Kramer vs Kramer.

We agreed to stay in touch.

The next time I heard from him was on New Year's Eve. He warned me to avoid Sarah Goodson.

SEAN: She is evil incarnate.

I hadn't seen Sarah since grade school. She was a cute, wee slip of a girl. Sweet and smart and about as evil as a petunia.

SEAN: Sarah made a pact with the devil. Do not let her into your life with her fake smiles and bullshit promises. She's a cokehead too. You cannot under any circumstances believe a word she says.

I promised Sean I would heed his warning and wished him a Happy New Year.

There were a few more late-night manic phone calls before I found the courage to tell him to stop calling. I didn't need that kind of cray cray in my life. At the time I was teaching fifteen yoga classes a week, cobbling together an acting career, raising a teenager, and nurturing a new relationship.

When he started posting racist and misogynist jokes on Facebook, it was the perfect excuse for me to sever all ties. I didn't hear hide nor hair until the following popped up on my Facebook feed:

Sean Reubens. Gone too soon.
April 12, 1968 – April 30, 2020
It is with great sadness, that I write to announce the
passing of a dear soul. Sean was a generous friend.
He was a funny, entertaining, passionate debater. He
was a creative person. A songwriter. A musician. A
theologian. He was interested in people. He always

wanted to make people feel good, laugh, and was hap-
piest when he spent time with friends and family and
made them smile.
As many of you may know, Sean struggled with
addiction most of his adult life. Sadly, he lost his battle
with this struggle on Thursday, April 30, 2020.
Sean will be deeply missed.
We love you Sean. ...

It's important to note that this was posted by 'Sarah Goodson,' who I'm happy to add is still as evil as a petunia.

8

LABEL THIS

I T WAS THE EIGHTIES and labels meant everything. We were living in a material world. Thanks, Madonna. My mom could not afford to dress me in designer duds. Every time she took on a part-time job her welfare cheque would be adjusted, making it impossible to get ahead. Even though we lived at the corner of Bad and Ass, the "rich folk" lived only a block or two away. Living so close to the working middle class made our differences embarrassingly obvious. I really just wanted to blend in. I had started babysitting and at $2.50 an hour—even my limited math skills told me that was a heck of a l-o-o-o-ong time to save for a $70 pair of jeans. I preferred the instant gratification of buying the latest Judy Blume. As a result, my wardrobe consisted mostly of flea market finds and a few select items from Bargain Harold's.

God almost came through for me that Christmas. Mom handed me a gift-wrapped box that was just the right size and weight. I ripped it open and pulled out a brand new pair of jeans! The stitching, the zipper, the intense inky blue all exactly the same as the jeans worn by my junior high peers! I turned them around to admire the pockets. There it was. The label, 'J-O-R-D-A-S-S.' JordASS? Not Jordache? Not Jordache. I tried unsuccessfully to hide my disappointment. Too late. Mom had to go all the way downtown and fight through the crowd of immigrants to find those pants and I better bloody well wear them. I did. They were tight and new. That's all that mattered, especially the tight part. I asked God to forgive me and promised Him I would wear them with long shirts so as not to expose my pro-creational assets. HE didn't need to know the truth in that I just wanted to hide the label. My favourite and only long shirt was from Tops 'n' Trends.

Tops 'n' Trends was a Canadian clothing line sold at house parties. Every item had the option of coming with an iron-on decal. There was a huge catalogue of images and expressions to choose from. My mom hosted two of these parties. Dad came to her first one. He bought me a shirt with a picture of a little boy holding a sign that said, "Kid for Rent Cheap." I liked it. It made everyone laugh and it was sparkly. He picked out two pairs of underwear for himself. One said, "Home of the Whopper," and the other said, "Rub Here and Get Three Wishes."

Fast forward a few years to the next Tops 'n' Trends party, Dad had moved out. Just as well. These parties were for girls. Because I was older I got to help Mom prep the snacks. We wrapped pickles in bologna for our version of pigs-in-blankets. We had celery with "Cheese Wuz" too. It tasted the same as Whiz but Wuz was a brighter orange and 20 cents cheaper! It was also my job to rake the shag carpet before and after the guests arrived. Another change at this party was I was allowed to choose my own shirt! I poured over the catalogue for hours until I finally chose a baseball T with blue sleeves and a grey body. My next choice was what numbers to pick. Having never played a team sport nor even followed one for that matter, I was at a loss. I knew I wanted something unique, something that would stand out.

I put a lot of thought into my choice of numbers and felt pretty pleased with myself, until I wore my new shirt to school. Turns out '00' was not perceived with the same open-mindedness with which it was designed. Yes my shirt was trendy and yes it covered my Jord-A-S-S but having '00' on my slow-to-grow chest did not catapult me into the upper echelons of the in-crowd. It had quite the opposite effect. I was now a double zero—double loser. Too bad. I wore it anyway and prayed even harder. This time I wasn't asking God for new clothes, I was pleading with him to give me boobs.

9

POTENTIAL

THE TV WAKES ME UP in the morning and puts me to sleep at night. Except for weekends when Mom takes a break from the "only goddamn pleasure she has left" and plays records instead. Her and the boyfriend-of-the-week split a 2-4 of Blue and a bottle of Smirnoff. If my dad hasn't picked me up, I join the party and sing and dance to Alice Cooper, the Stones and Supertramp. They love it. They love me. I can tell. They're clapping and laughing. If I can just keep them happy long enough maybe they won't fight. But bedtime always comes. I lie there waiting for the first smack of flesh, the sound of glass smashing, furniture breaking, and finally Mom calling me to help her.

Weekends with Dad are a different kind of action-adventure. He actually takes me places, like the Zoo, the Science Centre, museums, and the library. We eat out all the time too cuz he doesn't own any dishes. He moves a lot and only works when he feels like it. Mom says he spends all his money on beer and lottery tickets. Sometimes he gets lucky and finds a girlfriend who's got her own place. Like now his girlfriend, Evie, has this really cool apartment with tons of clothes and makeup cuz she's an actress and she doesn't mind me playing dress up with all her stuff. I find her lingerie collection. Handfuls of silky lace pieces. Each one a mystery. I try them all on wishing I had boobs to fill them but still liking the feeling they give me. I keep my favourite set on, underneath my cords and sweatshirt and go to the living room.

ME: Dad, Evie? Sit down on the couch okay. STAY there! Don't move.

My dad was beaming. Evie rolled her eyes. What now?

ME: I want to show you something.

I run over to the record player and put on Chris de Burgh's "Patricia the Stripper."

My audience sat quietly while I spun and bounced and threw my pants and shirt off to reveal the beautiful matching bra and panties set—Tah-Dah!!!

DAD: Whoa!!! Hubba Hubba Ding Dong!

EVIE: Where'd you learn that?!

ME: I don't know.

DAD: You're only ten years old for Christ sake!

ME: Eleven.

DAD: How do you know that shit?

ME: Once there was a stripper on Happy Days. She wore a mask but she was like pretty and mysterious.

DAD: Evie! Did you see that?! That's my kid!!

EVIE: Your kid in my lingerie.

ME: The Fonz fell in love with her but they couldn't get married cuz she wouldn't quit her job and–

DAD: Just like her mother, all sexed up nowhere to go.

ME: And she had to travel a lot.

Later that night Evie's director friend, Richard, came over. He brought a box of wine and a fake British accent.

RICHARD: Are you a dancer, Karen?

ME: Carrie.

RICHARD: You hold yourself like a dancer. Tall, elegant, lithe.

DAD: Yeah! Carrie's got a lithe little show for you. Don't ya Carrie?

I freeze.

DAD: Carrie! I'm talking to you! Do your little peeling thing for our guest, sweetie.

EVIE: Tony, I don't think that's a–

DAD: Come AWWWWWNNN! Carrie's gonna entertain you with a striptease dance like ya know.

RICHARD: Fabulous!

DAD: Oh, it's fabulous alright! You ready?

ME: No.

RICHARD: Perhaps Carol needs a cup of courage.

DAD: Carrie, wanna shot of wine?

ME: No.

DAD: No, what?

ME: No, thank you. I don't like that cheap shit.

I bolted, locked myself in the bedroom and gave myself makeovers. Sometimes I wonder if my life would have been different if I had danced for that director guy. Could I have been discovered ... as an actor? Then sometimes I wonder if my life would have turned out differently if I hadn't shown such ... potential.

10

ODD DUCK INDEED

H E READ OMNI MAGAZINES and was a fan of Genesis, Yes, and Rick Oldfield. He brought some good music into our house. He also brought a lot of Southern Comfort—the oxymoron of liquor.

I wanted to like him. He was my uncle's friend and I loved my uncle. Uncle was cool and funny as hell.

Mitchel Cooper was in his mid-20s when he hooked up with my then thirty-plus-year-old mom. He wore suits at first, ill-fitting suits over his tall puffy frame. These suits were supposed to make him look like he had an important job. Instead these suits made him look like he was going to small claims court. He also carried a briefcase. He carried a briefcase, yet I don't recall him ever being employed.

At first he was the perfect gentleman. He would arrive in a car borrowed from his brother Dave and take my mom on dates to fancy restaurants like the Fisherman Wharf or The Organ Grinder. Pretty soon his giant leatherette loafers had their own space at the door and his bottle of Brut was left on the bathroom counter.

On the nights when he wasn't at our place he stayed at his mom's and watched over his aunt. Aunt Cindy was severely mentally and physically handicapped. She spent her days babbling while looking at Sears catalogs. She was a lot nicer than Mitch's mom, Connie. Connie told me I would probably have a big ass when I grew up. "You better stay in school cuz you won't always be this pretty."

Connie also said she was a natural born salesperson. She sold Avon, Amway, and Regal products. Her little apartment in Mississauga was filled to the rafters with boxes of merchandise and cigarette smoke.

Mom said Mitch was an odd duck but basically a good person. I agreed with her on the first part. He peeled the white stuff off of an orange with a razor blade. He kept a stash of razor blades in his briefcase. The orange peeling ritual was time consuming. Mom said, "'It's a good thing you don't have to hurry off to work. You'd never get there on time."

He was also very phlegmy and would spit into a Kleenex, fold it in half, then in half again. He repeated this process, spit, fold, fold, over and over again until he had constructed a tiny Kleenex cube of concealed phlegm. He often neglected to throw them in the garbage which drove Mom nuts.

They fought a lot, especially when they drank together (which was every weekend). If I wasn't with Dad, I'd do my best to plan sleepovers at my friends' places. My stomach would twist itself sick with dread as the week approached Friday.

Their punch 'em up, drag down brawls sometimes ended in noisy make up sex. Oftentimes it ended with Mitch leaving. Mom or the cops would kick him out or he would storm out on his own. I prayed hard this meant we'd never see him again. I wanted Mom all to myself. I wanted my stomach to feel better and to have a good night's sleep.

Many years passed before that prayer was answered. He always returned, petulant and silent. He would slump in 'his' chair and refuse to speak or take off his parka. His khaki parka zipped tight. The fur trimmed hood did not conceal his hanging dog jowls. He'd sit silently and motionless, locked inside his old winter coat for hours.

One New Year's Eve when I was 11 or 12, Mom went to a party and left Mitch at home to babysit me. I spent the first part of the evening at the Middels eating oliebollen, a Dutch deep-fried donut. These sweet and greasy balls were a big deal as the Middel menu was otherwise healthy and frugally rationed. They busted out the oliebollen only on December 31 and we were allowed to have as many as we wanted. I begged to sleep over that night but I was denied. After stuffing my face with Dutch donuts I reluctantly walked the hallway home.

Mitch bought me something from Becker's. It was in a paper bag. It looked like it might be a Mad magazine! I Loved Mad or even its cheaper cousin, Cracked; they'd keep me occupied for a few hours. I said thanks and then excitedly reached inside the bag and pulled out a … Playgirl magazine. I stared at the cover. I stared at Mitch. I didn't know what was more shocking: to be holding a porn magazine or to have been given a porn magazine by Mom's boyfriend.

"It's okay. We don't have to tell your mom."

"You should give this to her. She'll probably like it."

I flipped through the pages and made some goofy jokes about their orange skin and steroid muscles. My face was burning but I tried my hardest to play it cool. Meanwhile I was praying for God to forgive me for looking at sinful images.

Minutes later, the ball dropped. Happy people on the TV kissed, cried, and celebrated a brand new start.

We stared at the TV screen, side by side on the couch, both wondering why she had left us alone on New Year's Eve.

11

LOVES BABY TENDER PIZZA VITTLES

EVERYONE ELSE WAS DOING IT. Why not me? They made it look easy, dangerous, and fun. I wanted in on the action. I told Mom. She agreed. We would host my first boy/girl party. Desperate to throw out my goody two shoes, I envisioned wildly dancing to rock 'n' roll, and kissing our faces off with an endless round of spin the bottle. You only turn 13 once! The Party of the Century was going to be held in our basement. The basement was a dark cinder block square. It's where we did laundry and our four leggeds did their business. Even though Mom was a clean freak, scented clumping kitty litter had yet to be invented. She tried to mask the smell with every caustic cleaner known to man. As a result, the basement smelled like a petting zoo held in a hospital wing .

"Make Love, Not War," was the first thing visible from the top of the stairs. My folks moved to 559 The West Mall in 1969. Their housewarming do was a basement painting party. Hearts, flowers, and peace signs adorned every surface. Kind of cool, but if I was going to impress the peers, this hippy den needed to be brought into the eighties. Armed with a can of Ultramarine, I set out to do a feature wall. Blue was my favourite colour. This was going to look rad! Not. Have you ever tried painting concrete? With a brush?! Ugh. Results were less than stellar. Undeterred, I tacked album covers to the wood support beams and strung up records across the rafters. A bed sheet hung in the corner served to hide the cat box while it also created a private make-out room.

The Kool-Aid was stirred, Pizza Pizza had been called, and the Loves Baby Soft had been sprayed. All that was left to do was wait for the guests to arrive. I hoped Blake Sewell wouldn't be upset I hadn't invited him. I didn't want him to think I still liked him. I mean I liked him. I just didn't like him like him. We went around together in grade 7. He had large hazel eyes, and a ski-slope nose. Sometimes we'd walk home from school together and he'd give me a quick peck at the street corner before tearing off for home. We barely talked. Neither of us had a clue what to do. The whole affair lasted 12 days.

I was hungry for more experiences, more kisses especially. That's not to say I was a total newbie. Back in kindergarten, I had the hots for a kid named Kevin, and I was not subtle about it. If he chose the sandbox during free-play time, I chose the sandbox. If he chose the water table or the craft centre I was right behind him. Wherever he was, I was in his face demanding we build a fort. Once we were cozied up in our little love nest, I suggested we play boyfriend and girlfriend, meaning we had to kiss, and kiss like they did in the movies not like how our aunties kiss us.

One day the teacher announced Kevin was moving and this would be his last day at Broadacres. Instead of crying like a soon to be abandoned lover, I took revenge. If Kevin could hurt me so easily, I would give him a taste of his own medicine. Scotty was my next target, a mop-top ginger with fascinating freckles. I followed poor Scotty like an imprinted gosling. Forget the fort. I made him kiss me right there by the swings, the slide, the teeter totter, all in plain view of Kevin.

Kevin, who was supposed to explode in a jealous rage and pronounce his undying love for me, happily steered a Hot Wheels through the dirt.

My sexual predator prowess didn't stop with the boys. I liked girls too. One day I convinced Dee Dee to drop her underwear and show me her thing. I only wish it was that straightforward. It wasn't. I added a whole other layer of creepiness. There was a cardboard room divider in front of the dress-up box in the House Play Station. I took a pencil and poked a hole in the room divider and convinced Dee Dee to drop trou while I watched through the hole. I then insisted we swap places too. It was only fair. I wanted to see if it was just as thrilling to be watched as it was to be the watcher. Where did this whole, hole voyeur/exhibitionist idea come from? Porky's hadn't even been released yet.

Hosting a party was a risky undertaking. I was not part of the 'in' crowd. What if no one showed up? What if I was destined to forever be on the bottom rung of the social status ladder? I had only recently burst out of my Born-Again-Christian bubble. Geraldine and her family moved to Bramalea. Tagging along to church events or sharing in their daily prayer sessions were no longer options. Her leaving meant I was free to not only hang with the cool kids but, God willing, maybe even become one!

To my great surprise and relief, almost everyone invited showed up. They filed in, said polite things to Mom, and then ran down the stairs to party central. The boys sat on one side. The girls sat on the other. No one said a word. Funny how your senses become more acute when you're nervous. I swore not only could I smell the cat pee but I could also detect Tender Vittles Seafood Medley in their poop. At least my pits didn't stink. They were soaked but so far my Secret was living up to its name. The silence was killing me though. I was always that kid at school who would be the first to answer the teacher's questions. I didn't care if I was right or wrong. I just couldn't handle the discomfort of a pause.

Seconds before shouting out, "'Let's play truth or dare!" the pizza arrived. We attacked the food like wolves on a rabbit. Once stuffed with greasy cheesy goodness, we dropped Thriller on the turn table. Chris Rouse was the first to dance. He could moonwalk better than MJ himself. He also fancied himself a lady's man. When he met Mom at the door he told her she was beautiful and kissed her hand.

We danced, we sang, we spun the bottle! There's nothing like a game of 'forced' kissing to reveal who likes who. Everyone pretends to be grossed out at first but as the game progresses the kisses get longer, the giggling stops, and all eyes become fixated on the bottle willing it to stop at the desired recipient. I kissed a couple of duds before the bottle pointed to my crush of the minute.

Mark Kooting was a tall shaggy blond with a subtle lisp. I figured because he was sweet and non-threatening, that God would be okay with us making out. It had been a few weeks since I'd gone to church and I was already backsliding into lustful ways. My fear of roasting in hell was at odds with the hormonal holocaust happening in my loins.

What happened next is easiest explained in a poem... maybe?

Thin necked glass clatters to a stop.
He jangles his limbs over to my
Shaking and slips me the tongue.
I inhale his Clearasil and flee the scene of the slime
Floating up and away
Clinging to the cobwebs in the rafters
I see all from above
But feel nothing
Except
Grandpa's lap from years ago
And his hands
He's missing three fingers, y'know.
Did you lose them in the war, Grandpa?
"Yeah it was a bloody war alright, and the lawnmower
won."
With only seven digits he played the piano, the accordion
and
Me.
He taught himself the national anthem of every
European country.
They all sounded the same.
Was it because of his missing fingers or had he too many
rye and gingers under his open belt?
"Guess this one Care, CARE, CARRIE!!! Are you listen-
ing?!"
Russia?
"Jesus Christ. It's not bloody Russia. It's Poland.
Lambchop. Poland
Come 'ere. Come HERE! Let Grandpa teach you a ditty."
And he did. He taught me Baa Baa Black Sheep.
And how to get out of dodge, without moving a muscle.

From my vantage point up above I could tell Mark Kooting was nervous. Yet he was so gentle. Why couldn't I participate? It's like I wasn't even invited to my own party. I could see everyone talking and laughing but my ears were stuffed with cotton. My head was full of helium drifting further away from the action below.

I'm not sure exactly when I returned to me. It was sometime before the parents came to collect their kids. I remember everyone had grape-stained smiles on their faces when they left. There was lots of giggling too. It must have been a success!

Lying in bed that night, I rewound the tape of the day's events. The best part was eating pizza. Everything else made me feel like a dirty girl. I turned to the Bible, and scoured the scriptures for something comforting. When that didn't work I prayed as hard as I could. "Dear God. I'm so very sorry. I hope you can find it in your heart to forgive me for straying. I've learned my lesson and I promise to not let anyone French kiss me again until I am at least 18. Just please, please, please make that scary-disappearing-act-thing, stop. Thank you. In Jesus' name I pray. Amen."

12

ERNEST, EARNEST? HARDLY

EVERY NOVEMBER 11 we are reminded to never forget those who gave the ultimate sacrifice to ensure our freedoms. For me that means remembering my grandpa, Ernest Moyle. He wasn't the only person in the family who fought in a war but he talked about it as if he were the only one that mattered.

Always the dutiful daughter, Mom would call her dad on November 11 and thank him for his service.

Ernie appreciated the gesture but that did not mean she or anyone else was off the hook when it came to attending the annual veterans' parade. It was held every Labour Day on the Exhibition grounds.

Mom, Aunt Doreen, Uncle Herb, Cousin Tammy and I wedged ourselves in the stands under the heat of a dying summer and cheered on the patriarch of our clan, as he limped alongside the other remaining survivors from his battalion. We sweated it out as an endless parade of seniors, stiff with sanctimony, arthritis, and rye, crawled past in quasi precision. Occasionally the monotony was broken by a soldier in a wheelchair and I got excited remembering that there were bumper cars on the other side of this parade of sadness. I just had to be patient and then make lots of noise when Grandpa came into view. It was always an emotional day for Ernie. Was that a single tear rivering its way down his jowl and pooling on top of his chins? His shirt was too tight. Could he breathe okay? Why was his face so pale? How could a nose be that red? It was unsettling to see him vulnerable. He was the master of his home. The cock of his roost. He held court in his basement bar and was head of the table at all family dinners. When he spoke we listened. When he told a racist joke we were expected to laugh. He hated anyone who was not white, including Italians and Latinos. In 1982, when the Italians beat Germany in the FIFA Cup, his predominantly Italian neighbourhood erupted in boisterous celebration. Ernie was having none of it. He took it upon himself to "Teach those greasy wops a lesson!" A glass of rye in one hand and a gun in the other he took to his driveway screaming and shooting at the filthy immigrants to go back to where they came from. Fortunately his aim was compromised and no one was hit. He was charged with 'being a cranky old drunk with bad aim.' As punishment he was ordered to surrender his firearm collection. Unfortunately he engaged in other stealthier crimes that would never be brought to justice.

We tried to out him when I was 11 and Cousin Tammy was 8. It was a hot summer night around a campfire. It was just us girls. Aunt Doreen had rented a one-room cabin on Buckhorn Lake. She invited me and Mom to stay with them for a few days. My cousin and I always had fun together. Even though she was three years younger, we were more like sisters who happened to like each other. Of course, being older, I was the bossy one; yet it was actually Tammy's idea to tattle on Grandpa. I was scared but my gut knew it was the right thing to do. We started off by telling them that Grandpa liked to kiss us with an open mouth. They said, "Yeah, he likes sloppy kisses. Just turn your head next time." We went on to explain that when we slept at his place he crawled into bed with us and pretended he was a big dog who licked and sucked our toes. Then he would tickle us until we couldn't breathe and he would rub us 'down there' or try to stick his hands down our pants when he sat on the piano bench with us. I didn't tell them about the time he made me put my mouth on his thing. They were crying hard by this point. I hated seeing Mom upset. Aunt Doreen said she wasn't surprised. He did things to her all the time up until she left home. Mom swore he never touched her. Or maybe she couldn't remember. It's possible the electric shock therapy that was used to treat her 'partial schizophrenia' caused some memory loss. We comforted our moms and apologized for making them cry.

Not a word was said to Grandpa about his inappropriate behaviour. It was as if our big tell-all sob-fest had never happened. We carried on as before, showing up for all the holiday dinners and birthday celebrations. I gave him a wider birth and made sure we were never alone together. By the time I was 11, he lost interest in me. I remember the moment clearly.

The family was gathered in his backyard. He was standing beside one of his brothers. They all looked alike so I never bothered to learn who was who. He asked me to go make him a drink.

Cha-Cha, go bring your Poppa a rye and ginger.

No.

The veins in his nose filled with blood. There was a tremor in his waddle. Go get me a drink, Lambchop. I looked him in the eye, shook my head and walked away. I could hear him swearing. Did he just call me an ungrateful bitch?

13

I'M GOING TO LIVE FOREVER

THE PRESSURE WAS ON in grade 8 to enroll in the appropriate high school. I didn't see myself fitting in to either of the two designated schools in my neighbourhood. Vincent Massey was notoriously bad ass. I was the opposite. My sensitivity would have been like chum in a shark tank. Silverthorn Collegiate was where all the middle-upper class kids went. They would be sure to bully me for my church basement finds and knockoff Jord-Ass jeans.

I needed a fresh start at a school far from the corner of Bad and Ass.

Enter The Etobicoke School of the Arts. It had opened the year prior and was a good 45-minute bus ride away. It was also a haven for freaks, geeks, misfits, and dreamers. Perfect for me but what was I supposed to major in? The logical choice would have been music. I was a cellist for the junior high orchestra even though I had no clue how to read music and Mom said the sound of me practicing was like listening to an old cat being tortured. I needed a hell of a lot more encouragement if I were going to lug that thing on the TTC every day. Music was out, as was Visual Art and Dance. I loved them both but didn't think I was good enough to pursue either. The only major left was Drama. I already had a lot of practice pretending to be Sandy from Grease, Kelly Garrett from Charlie's Angels, or a happy kid from The West Mall and Rathburn Road. It was settled. I would audition for the Etobicoke School of the Arts (ESA), Theatre Department.

How hard could it be? According to the registration package, all I had to do was prepare a two-minute monologue.

Thanks to the school library, I not only learned that a monologue was a speech written for a singular actor, I also found the piece that was sure to win me a spot at ESA. It was a modern comedic piece about an anxious girl on prom night. Preparation consisted of reading it into a hairbrush in front of a mirror and watching multiple episodes of Fame – the TV series. By the time my audition slot rolled around I was ready to light up the sky like a flame!

There were three adjudicators sitting at a table facing the stage.

I climbed up and looked down at them while politely answering their questions. This was the interview component of the audition. We discussed my previous acting experience and I told them I was Blitzen in the kindergarten Christmas pageant. They asked what monologue I was going to do. And what it was from.

"Her name is Marcia, and it's from this book," I said while holding up a copy of Monologues for Young Actors.

Whenever you're ready.

I took a deep breath and read to my audience of three. They were silent throughout. When I was finished I let them know by saying, "The end."

Did I bow? I might have bowed.

JUDGE #1: Okay.
JUDGE #2: How about you do it again but this time without reading from the book in your hands.
ME: What do you mean?
JUDGE #3: Do the piece again by memory.

JUDGE #1: That's how monologues are done.

ME: Oh.

JUDGE #2: If you forget some words just make them up!

JUDGE #3: And do it as if you were a frog.

ME: A frog?

JUDGE #2: Yes. Whenever you're ready.

I took a deep squat with knees and toes pointing out to the sides.

Surprisingly the words came easy. I punctuated the text with a couple of ribbits, eliciting a polite chuckle.

It was the following line that landed me in the winner's circle—

Instead of, "If Danny doesn't ask me to dance I will die," I said, "If Danny doesn't ask me to dance, I will croak. I'll simply croak."

They laughed and it felt like a warm hug.

Thus began my lifelong search for applause, adoration, and paying gigs.

14

ALL INCLUDED

I T'S NOT A COMMUNIST COUNTRY. Just sounds like one," he said as he threw four tickets on the kitchen table.

What was he even doing here?

I was shocked to see my dad.

If he came by at all, it was on a Friday to take me to his place for the weekend. This was a school night. As if that wasn't weird enough, he was also sober.

DAD: Lady at the travel place said it's the next Jamaica.
Mom looked at him sideways.
MOM: Where did you get the money from?
He threw a handful of bills on the table.
DAD: Get yourself some beach clothes, a big towel, and a bag to put all your shit in.
She can't let it go.
MOM: What did you do, Tony, rob a bank?
DAD: Christ Lorraine. It's Anton. Call me Anton.
I look at him with a smirk.
ME: Did you use a gun, Dad?
DAD: I got lucky at the racetrack Schmool. Call Naomi. Make sure her parents are copacetic.

My bestie Naomi was just as shocked and excited as me. Dad talked with her mom on the phone and reassured her, No, he didn't want any money. His treat.

The only other time I had been on a plane was when I was 8. Oma took me to the Fatherland to show me off to her family. During my month-long stay, I learned how to sprecken zie Deutsch, sniff snuff and slurp schnapps. Everyone spoiled me rotten and I lapped it up. I came home fatter, stuffed with the comfort of learning that normal happy people weren't just characters on TV but they actually existed in my very own family. Too bad they lived an 8-hour flight away.

ME: How long is the plane ride, Dad?

DAD: Four hours and five minutes. We leave at 8:00 a.m. and get there at noon but it'll be 1:00 there cuz of the time zones.

MOM: Do they have a beach?

DAD: It's a goddamn island, Lorraine. Whaddya think?

MOM: I'm not swimming in no ocean. I seen what happened in Jaws. No way. Nope. No thank you.

ME: Oh my God. I've always wanted to swim in the ocean!

DAD: It's in the Caribbean. Everyone speaks Spanish. It's where Columbus landed. Ripe with history there.

Both of them are smoking like it'll make our departure date come quicker.

DAD: Brand new hotel. We're getting it all-included.

MOM: I better have my own bed. I'm not sleeping with you.

DAD: I got two rooms with two queen size beds in each room. The kids in one and us in the other.

MOM: Great. Do you still grind your teeth, Tone?

DAD: Do you still snore, Lore?

Couple of comedians these two. They were also a couple of professional piss tanks. I was worried. Their sniping banter was all fun and games now, but what would happen when unlimited piña coladas were poured into the mix?

Dad was a Jekyll and Hyde drunk. The night would begin with his lavishing his drinking buddies with praise and bear hugs. He was everyone's best friend. Even the wary ones were won over once he bought them enough drinks. He told the crudest jokes, challenged the men to arm wrestle, and the women to punch him in the gut as hard as they could. He could light a match and open a beer off any surface, including his teeth. Other party tricks involved tossing a smoke in the air and catching it with his mouth (filter end in, of course), lighting his farts on fire, or, in more genteel company, he sucked the butane out of a zippo and turned his mouth into a blowtorch. Inevitably this one-man circus would take an abrupt 180 turn. The twinkle in his eye would be replaced with a darkness so deep you'd be wishing for a flashlight to make a swift exit. This volatile flip of the switch triggered a "danger ahead" sign. Unfortunately Mom wasn't much of a reader. She saw no reason to hide from Mr. Hyde. Anton's demons did not scare her. They pissed her off. In her blurry eyes, the appearance of Mr. Hyde meant the party was over and Mom never wanted the party to end. She took the Beastie Boys lyrics literally; you gotta fight for your right to party! And fight she did.

It wasn't uncommon for her to throw the first punch while Dad was driving us home from a boozy visit with Aunt Doreen or the grandparents.

To this day the site of the Holiday Drive exit onto The West Mall, lodges a white-cold brick in my throat. The familiar shivering begins and I see Dad steering with his left hand and slapping Mom with his right. I yell at them to stop. They don't hear me. I am invisible. It will only get worse once we're home and he has both hands free. My stomach hurts. It will only get worse. I will be sent to bed. I will brush my teeth. Choo Choo, Schultz, and Brandy will cower in bed with me. We will not sleep; we will pray it will stop before there is too much blood. I will be the first up. I will empty ashtrays, pick up broken glass, and eat Shreddies while watching cartoons. When the parental units get up, no one will talk about the night before. Mom will want the couch for the day and Dad might take me to Centennial Park where we'll watch the paragliders soar like birds over Etobicoke.

OUR TRIP TO THE DOMINICAN REPUBLIC went well. Miraculously there were no brawls! Dad wasn't around enough to fight. He rented a motorbike and spent the days exploring the island and the nights getting to know 'its senoritas'. Mom parked it poolside. Naomi fought off the attention of locals who had never seen a 'cheena' before. In Etobicoke she was just another third-generation Japanese kid. In the Dominican Republic, she was an exotic Eastern star who everyone either feared or wanted to touch. I was envious of her and all the attention she garnered. She was better at everything. Better marks, better artist, better dancer, better body. She even tanned better than me. I got burned so badly that I woke up with my eyes swollen shut behind big bubbly blisters. We raced to the local clinic. Mom was freaking out, and I felt special for a few minutes. The nurse shook her head, handed us a couple of creams to treat my second-degree burns and gave me strict orders, "No go in sun!"

Dad bought me the biggest brimmed hat he could find. It was also the ugliest. This monstrosity could be seen from space was made out of banana leaves and looked like the lid of a garbage can. If nothing else I was finally getting more attention than Naomi, that is until Dad propositioned her.

That's right. He volunteered his services as a sex instructor, a Mr. Robinson, a titillation tutor. Once Naomi turned 18, of course. "Young guys don't know what they're doing. I know my way around the female body. I've had a lot of experience. You sleep with people your age, you're going to regret it. They won't know how to pleasure you. Those young punks will just take what they want. They don't care about your needs. A mature gentleman like myself, we're different. We know. We take our time. A few sessions with me and you'll learn shit that'll make your head spin faster than that chick from the Exorcist. "

Always the academic, bent on self-improvement, Naomi seriously considered his offer.

Wrong as it may be, I was proud of my dad. Proud that he had something of value to offer my best friend.

I also liked that they had a special bond. This new pact secured Naomi's position in my life. We would have to remain close until she was 18, giving us another four years together!

15

RAW

MARILYN WAS A BONEY BEAUTY, all braces and other expensive accessories. She was a true blond with barely there eyebrows and white eyelashes framing pale blue eyes. She was shiny and clean as if dipped daily in a vat of bleach. Dirt could not stick to her. It was obvious she came from the good part of Etobicoke. Yet, we liked one another. I think it's because we were both drama queens prone to dark emoments and we had a crush on the same boy. We just had to have a sleepover to solidify our bond. It took a lot of whining, begging and bartering for Marilyn to convince her parents to allow her to sleep over at my place. They were worried and rightfully so. Our projects looked as rough as they were. Marilyn must have put on an Oscar-worthy performance. They consented!

When Friday rolled around, I started to get nervous, simply because it was Friday. Ever since I was a little kid, Fridays stirred up feelings of dread. Would Dad show up? Would he send a taxi for me? Would Mom let me get in the taxi? She swore never again. Usually he took the TTC and I'd wait for him at the bus stop in front of our house. More often than not he was a no show. I would be left crying on the sidewalk clutching a grocery bag full of library books and a toothbrush. My mom did her best to console me. She hated seeing me hurt by him and she hated him for ruining her weekend. She usually had plans to go out, and now she was stuck trying to find a last-minute babysitter she could afford. They were almost impossible to come by. The ones she did manage to hire are worthy of their own scary chapter. If no one was available, that meant the party was happening in unit 204. Not the appetizers, cocktails, and games kind of party but the drink, break stuff, and hurt people kind of party. This was usually a party of two, just Mom and whomever she was seeing at the time.

None of these concerns mattered on the Friday night of Marilyn's sleepover. I was in grade 9! I was doing my own babysitting thank you very much. Dad was missing in action. We hadn't heard from him in months. As far as party time went, I didn't have to stress about that either. Mom and Mitch, her boyfriend of four years, were 'taking a break.' Still, my guts were churning. Old habits die hard, I guess.

When Marilyn arrived she had a polite exchange with Mom and then we disappeared into my room. We gave each other makeovers, manicures, and new hairdos. The entire time we talked and giggled non-stop. Our mutual crush was called and hung up on. Secrets were shared and pinky swears were made. We were bonding. The sleepover was a success!

Then Mitch showed up. He most likely came to the door pleading that he just wanted to talk. Mom let him and his brown bag of booze inside.

I don't know how much time had passed before he called for me to come downstairs. I do know that what I'm about to recount happened very quickly. I ran down the stairs. Mitch asked me if I knew that Mom had gone on a date last weekend. I answered his question with a straight face and zero attitude. I just wanted to get back to my room. Marilyn was waiting for me. I said, "Yeah. You guys are on a break, right?" Boom! He punches my face. "Slut! You fuckin' slut!" I don't know who he's yelling at. "Leave her alone!" Mom swings at him. He grabs her, grabs me, we pummel him with everything we have. I'm used to jumping on his back when he hits Mom but this is a first. He has never attacked me before. Being on the receiving end is way worse. It's like a nightmare where you're fighting a monster as hard as you can but the beast doesn't even flinch. He's fueled by jealous rage, liquor, and whatever other drug he scored on his way here. He pushes us both up against the wall and pins us there with the kitchen table. We can't move. I scream for Marilyn to call the cops. I may have blacked out. I may have disappeared to my happy place, at Oma's, swimming on Three Mile Lake. Sirens, flashing lights, chattering teeth, aching stomach, and a throbbing eye, bring me back. I am awake and fully feeling everything. Mitch is gone. Marilyn's parents have taken her home. Mom and I hold each other tight. She strokes my hair and says, "Never again, never again."

There was a restraining order put out on Mitch, which made things somewhat peaceful at 559 The West Mall. That is until she caved. Sadly, Mom was no different than most victims. She gave out second, third, and fourth chances like they were napkins on wing night. It wasn't long before Mitch was back to being a regular fixture in our home.

Mom was right about one thing. He never again laid a hand on me, well not a violent one that is.

16

UNFORGETTABLE MIKES

Growing up, I knew a lot of Mikes. There was Mike Vee-Oh with the opera-singing mom in unit 207. There was also Mike Hawk, who gave me my first tattoo. Schoolmates since grade one, he used to chase me and spit in my hair. According to Mom this meant he liked me. He was an adorable kid with long eyelashes and pouty lips that hid surprisingly perfect teeth. He eventually hardened up his cuteness with a perpetual smoke in his mouth and one behind each ear. By the time he was 14, he was selling drugs and giving poke and stick tattoos out of his attic bedroom in Mimico. I was crushing on him hard. To prove to him that I was no longer a creepy Christian, I let him tattoo three sixes on my right shoulder. Not only did Mike Hawk give me the mark of The Beast, a few years later he gave me a nasty case of genital warts.

Cousin Mike and Mom were close. He looked like his father, Mom's older brother, Ernie Junior. Ernie Jr. died in a motorcycle accident when Cousin Mike was just a kid. Mom and Cousin Mike would get together and drink and smoke until they cried about the great man who was Ernest Jr, father, brother, Elvis look alike, gone too soon. A couple times a year, Cousin Mike took the Greyhound bus from Fort Erie to Toronto to visit us. He always brought beer and some superior reefer he had picked up stateside. On this particular Labour Day long weekend, Cousin Mike suggested we needed hash to round out our party favours. Eager to please, I offered to dash over to a dealer friend who lived close by.

Mike Debussy was my Jim Morrison look-a-like crush. He was all soft brown curls and eyes that were never fully open. He lived in his parents' basement among a collection of records and dumbbells. There may have been a pet boa too. Or could that have been a hallucination? I did see his trouser snake once or twice.

On this particular afternoon I knock on his door with the singular mission of brokering a drug deal between the two Mikes.

ME: Hi Mike. How are you?
MIKE: (stands in doorway wearing tiny shorts) Hey.
ME: I'm fine thanks. Sorry to bother you but I was hoping you might have some hash I could buy from you?

It's only been a year since I ended my walk with Jesus and took up running with the devil. I was still more sweet than street. I was not too cool for school. I was a drama nerd dressed up like a hair band groupie. With my badass ink, playboy bunny t-shirt, and cut offs, one would think I would be a tad cooler. No. I talk a lot when I'm nervous. And Jim-Morrison-Mike with his hair and muscles and stoned-ness, made me very nervous.

ME: It's for my cousin whose name is also Mike—Ha! He's visiting my mom and me for the long weekend. He has money. That he gave to me. To give to you. How much is hash? I mean, how much hash can twenty dollars buy…these days?

Mike scratches his abs with one hand and his armpit with the other. He is thinking, processing my questions, calculating the math, or not.

MIKE: I only have acid. Purple Mikes. 4 for 20
ME: Could I be allowed to use your phone please?

Mike gives a slight nod and steps aside. I let myself into his kitchen and pick up the receiver from the yellow phone on the wall.

ME: Hi Mom. Can I please speak to Cousin Mike?

COUSIN MIKE: Hey Little C. Wassup?

ME: Bad news is he doesn't have any hash. The good news is he has acid! Should I buy some acid?

COUSIN MIKE: Yeah. Pick up four burgers on your way home too.

ME: He says the acid is five dollars per hit.

COUSIN MIKE: Cool. Bring back four burgers.

The transaction is made and I run back home excited to try acid for the first time.

COUSIN MIKE: Here's the deal Little C. Your Mom's gonna drop but she doesn't want you to know. She doesn't want you to drop either. So don't do anything weird. I left your hit under the TV Guide on the back of the toilet. Stay cool. She can't know you're tripping.

ME: She won't know a thing. I'm in theatre school. Remember!

I slipped into the bathroom and picked up the TV Guide. The Purple Mike was stuck on Tony Danza's forehead. With eyes squinted it looked like a Bindi. I giggle before placing the hit on my tongue. Who's the boss now, Tony?

The vibe in the living room was suppressed excitement and nervous anticipation. Cousin Mike and Mitch had dropped openly. Mom and I maintained the ruse of sober gatekeepers. Our job was to observe and assist with a safe landing if necessary. That lasted for the first 50 minutes before TAKE-OFF!!!

There we all were, on the same cosmic flight with no parachutes to be found. I took it upon myself to be the on board entertainment by choreographing a song and dance number. This piece accompanied a live demonstration on how to shave your legs with an electric razor. Mom appreciating a good show, vocalized her emotional range. One moment she was laughing hysterically, "Too funny. I- can't- breathe. My- cheeks- are- breaking!"

Seconds later she snapped into Mom mode, "Don't forget your knees, Care. You always forget to shave your knees." Followed by utter mortification, "Careful!!! You're going to cut your leg off!"

We locked eyes. Busted. Our secrets were revealed. Without a word we agree to not out one another. We were on this trip together. There was no turning back now. We continued our silent conversation for an eternity until Mom did what she always did when the quiet got too noisy; she turned on the television.

The Jerry Lewis Telethon was on. It was tradition to watch it every Labour Day weekend. The celebrity guest interviews, musical acts and stand-up comics made for good viewing. It was exciting too to watch the numbers climb as non-stop pledges came in. The fight to end muscular dystrophy was urgent and it was happening right there at the corner of Bad and Ass. A parade of children were wheeled on to the stage, designed to pull on the strings of the heart and purse. This was the part of the program that usually started Mom crying. If she cried, I cried. There was no way I could let myself cry. Not now. If I turned the taps on I wouldn't be able to turn them off. There would be a flood. I saw the living room fill with tears, washing over the furniture. Couch cushions and knickknacks float past. Our pets, Chew Chew, Brandy, and

Schultz, are in a dinghy sipping daiquiris. I start to giggle. All eyes move away from the TV and onto my laughing face. I point to the rising water in front of us. It looks like I'm pointing at the kids on the screen. "Move to higher ground," I want to say but I'm laughing too hard. Then it hits me: If I stay in this room I will drown. I will drown in my own tears. I have to leave. I cannot die here in this sad flood! There's an entire universe on the other side of these walls and it's calling me. "I have to go and explore the world," I proclaim while wading over to the door. Mom, looking fearful yet proud, pipes up with, "You've always been so much braver than me." Waving goodbye, I open the door and start running.

17

LEMON OPERA

THE HALLWAY was often thick with smoking teens trying to out-cool one another while brainstorming ways to score their next high. I was one of those teens. I fell hard to fit right in. I downplayed the un-cool stuff like how much I loved going to the Etobicoke School of the Arts as a drama major and a dance minor. Having potential was akin to having herpes. No one wanted to get close to that. The future was for losers.

Across the hall and three units down lived a Dutch woman and her son Michael. Their last name was Van-O-something but none of us could pronounce it properly. Even though we all had police records, we would have never addressed an adult by their first name. We were polite little thugs. Michael said we could call his Mom, Ms. Vee-Oh.

Ms. Vee-Oh was a tall, jaundiced diabetic who wore night-gowns and a long-suffering scowl. Her son Michael was my age. He was all she had or so she claimed. But I knew she also had a gift. She was an opera singer. We could hear her from inside our unit. What Mom called "bloody caterwauling," I found beautiful. I'd slip into the hallway and walk right up to Ms. Vee-Oh's door, and listen with my entire being. I had no idea what language she was singing in. All I know is it felt like she was singing for all the lost souls at 559 The West Mall.

Aside from this occasional operatic interlude, piss alley was a cacophony of domestic dramas. "You ate the last of the fuckin' cheeze wieners, ass wipe ! You don't need it anyway lard ass," OR "Why weren't you at school today? Look at me when I'm talkin' to you! You're gonna' end up just like your lousy goddamn father!" Add to this the thud of bodies hitting walls, glass smashing, and sitcom laughter and that about sums up the soundscape. I vowed to get out of there as soon as I finished school. In the meantime, there was no shortage of temporary escapes.

Lemon Gin was all the rage. The fact the bottle had a warning label that read, ""Overconsumption of Lemon Gin may cause temporary blindness" made me want to try it even more.

It was a Friday night, and a couple of acquaintances from my old elementary school invited me to their high school dance at Silverthorn Collegiate. I call them acquaintances because they wanted nothing to do with me when I was a Born Again Christian. But recently word had gotten out that I had stopped going to church and better yet, could pull booze. I was never asked for ID. It's not like I looked any older than my peers but I knew how to drop my voice, slow my gestures, and think 25. The acting classes were paying off.

We met at someone's house. Her name escapes me. At the time I thought she must be rich because she had an island in the kitchen. In the middle of the island was an extra-large pizza with a note, "For you and your friends. Enjoy!" Love Mom and Dad. Wow. She still had two parents. Everyone attacked the pizza except me. I was in the thick of my bulimic phase and this house was too pretty to throw up in. Besides, I was more interested in drinking than eating. Food would just dampen the buzz. I told the other girls I had already had dinner and started to swill the Lemon Gin straight from the bottle. Meanwhile we frosted the eyelids and competed to see who could sculpt the biggest bangs.

I've always found the prep for an event to be more fun than the event itself. It's the music, the banter, and the anticipation of the destination that stack up like a pile of Polaroids in the memory bank.

I remember tossing the empty mickey into some trees. I remember dancing in the school gym. I remember waking up from a deep nap in front of Silverthorn Collegiate. I remember hearing voices and the sound of the bass coming from inside the school. The dance wasn't over. But I was done. I started to make my way home. This was a well-lit neighbourhood. Why was it so dark? It took a long time, a very long time, to navigate an otherwise direct path to Bad and Ass. When I finally made it home, I dug deep into my purse, which was miraculously still strapped across my chest postman style; 35 cents, teal eyeliner, rolling papers, Bonnie Bell Watermelon Lip Smacker, a Bic pen, a Zippo I stole from Macs, a hairbrush, an unwrapped piece of Dentyne, and Jim Morrison's "No One Here Gets Out Alive." As I pick up each item I marvel at every detail. Colours, letters, words as if seeing them for the first time. Then it dawns on me. I know why it took so long to get home. I had experienced temporary blindness! Wicked. I couldn't wait to tell my friends. That is so hardcore! But wait. Shit. I forgot my keys. Oh no. I have to wake up my mom. Not so wicked. I knock tentatively, barely audible but loudly enough for Brandy to hear. She barks frantically. I shove the furry Dentyne in my mouth, and brace myself. I wait. Nothing. I wait until Brandy gets tired of the sound of her own bark. She sniffs the door one last time and then click, click, clicks away to her spot on the couch.

Mom must be at one of her boyfriends' houses. I begin a slow walk through the hallway, listening for sounds of life. It was unusually quiet for a Friday night. Must be later than I think. Finally faint strains of an infomercial can be heard from the Vee-Oh's unit. I work up the courage to knock. Ms. Vee-Oh opens the door. Her stained nightgown was a welcome sight. Actually just having sight at all was welcomed! I asked her what time it was.

"It's half past goddamn two in the morning. What the hell's wrong with you?" I told her I was blinded by Lemon Gin and it took me a couple of hours to walk home and now I'm locked out. She stared at me with such deep disappointment; I felt terrible. I had let her down. I was turning out just like all the rest.

"I love your singing," I blurt out. She closes the door slightly, hiding herself, but I keep going.

"I didn't think I liked opera but the way you sing it makes me like it a lot. It really brightens up the hallway." She opens the door and yells, "Michael, make some sandwiches, we're having a guest."

After eating the gooiest, thickest PB-n-J ever, which I keep in my stomach, I have the sleep of a thousand puppies. When I wake up, my head is a giant cowbell but I still manage to fold the Batman sheets Michael had made up the couch with. I tiptoe to the door and take a look back at their humble living room. I see the broken Lazy Boy stuck in mid recline and flash back to just hours earlier when I asked Ms. Vee-Oh to sing me a lullaby. She called me a crazy drunk but not before smiling first.

18

NORMAN

WHAT TELL-ALL GRITTY MEMOIR would be complete without a how I lost my virginity story. Hold up! I did not lose anything. Whoever came up with that expression 'lost' my virginity was deep into the shaming of women. To lose, implies a reckless forgetfulness. Damn! Where did I put my virginity? I could have sworn I just had it yesterday? Did I leave it at the bar, or maybe at Dollarama? Must retrace my steps.

To be clear, I did not lose my virginity. I surrendered it? I permitted Stormin' Norman entrance?

We had been making out for months in Leanna Worl's unit. She lived across the hall in #203. Her mom worked at Burger Boy and was never home. Leanna's older brothers were in jail so no one knew or cared that she was spending more time with her boyfriend Lee than she was at school. This is the same Leanna who taught me how to smoke in grade 1 and who had her cherry popped at 13. Mom was shocked. "That's too young. By the time she's 30 she'll have done everything and sex'll be boring. Virginity is like a cheap lawn chair. Once it's broken there's no fixing it." All our friends on The West Mall were doing it. I was the final holdout. Norman was a good candidate to have as my first. He was 17, a tall gaggle of freckled limbs. With big blue eyes, shaggy red hair and only one testicle, he was attractive without being intimidating. In fact if it weren't for the perpetual cigarette between his pouty lips, he could be considered quite pretty.

Our make out sessions were getting hotter and heavier.

Taking the next step was inevitable. I was more than ready to renounce my v-card.

It was a Saturday and Mom was out for the night.

Norm put on Def Leppard's Pyromania while I mixed us a couple of screwdrivers.

I was more excited than nervous for this maiden (head) voyage.

We threw back the drinks and started with our familiar deep tongue, teeth gnashing, face sucking. This time it was less a make-out marathon and more a warm-up stretch in preparation for the big event.

Gunter Glieben Glauten Globen!
And we were off.
There was much fumbling and grinding.
I kept my shirt on.
We hadn't played enough with my boobs to appreciate just how sensitive they were.
That discovery came later in life.

We got the power got the glory
Say you need it and if you need it say yeah
Say yeah

Our jeans lay tangled on the brown shag.

My little mutt, Brandy, sniffed them, glanced at me and licked her lips.

More sweating and stumbling.

I'm burning burning I got the fever
I know for sure there ain't no cure.
So feel it don't fight it go with the flow
Gimme gimme gimme gimme one more for the road

Is it in?
Yeah.
Ow!
UhhhhhGGHHhhhhggghhh!!!!!!
PAUSE
Is it done?
Yeah.
Sorry.
It's okay.
I'll be right back.

Norman got dressed and went across the street to the gas station. He brought me back a can of Orange Crush. I put my pants back on and then he took me to his unit where he made us fried-egg sandwiches. Kind of romantic, eh?

All and all it was as mom warned—like a cheap lawn chair. It very much collapsed under the weight of my expectations. The whole ordeal took four minutes—the length of Def Leppard's "Rock of Ages." While it may have been anticlimactic, it hardly ruined me for sex. On the contrary, I caught a glimpse of a world of possibilities. A world of which I was very eager to explore.

19

HEAT

I T WAS ONE of those relentlessly hot days that make you want to skip work and get drunk on a patio. I was only 16 so I did the next best thing.

We met at the bus stop a block away from school. He was a cute, rich, bad boy. Not my usual taste. I was more accustomed to the cute, poor, bad boys. K and I had partied together a couple of times. He was 20 and on the third year of his gap year. He had done the European backpack thing as well as a summer stint as a BC tree planter. He was worldly, handsome, and a source of some quality drugs not easily found at the corner of Bad and Ass.

He flashed a 6-figure smile and passed me a Styrofoam cup. I had no idea he was a tea drinker, and in this heat?! Totally rad. I took a big gulp as he explained that MDMA is a derivative of the peyote plant. This 'tea' promised a psyche-delic but happy experience. We climbed aboard.

The bus was taking us to my place. Mom was working days at Shoppers Drug Mart. We'd have the place to ourselves. Knowing we'd be naked in 20 minutes was a high all on its own. We chatted, giggled, and watched the stifling sameness of the suburban landscape slide past the windows. By the time we got off the bus the pavement was fluid. The dandeli-ons in the sidewalk cracks were afraid of us. I bent down to comfort them. K squeezed my hand and pulled me upright. "Let's get you inside." That was music to my ears, literally. His voice was a sitar, bending words that smelled of sandalwood.

My pets, Choo Choo, Shultz, and Brandy, greeted us at the door. We danced a jig with them before following the yellow brick road up to my bedroom. I opened the door to an Asian-inspired garden of delight, complete with giant fans, a futon and a rice paper room divider. This was not a hallucination. Thanks to my dad, I had a damn fine bedroom. That year he had mysteriously and quickly come into some cash and just as quickly and not so mysteriously was broke again. But that's another story.

We fell to the futon and peeled off the gift wrap of sticky summer clothes. We had been naked together before but this time we saw each other in a whole new kaleidoscopic light. The vee of hair on his chest was its own ecosystem with a small pond and eaglets. The large vee of hair between my legs held the secrets of womankind in its dark forest. He smelled like new leather and I, like baked goods. We made a feast of one another pausing only to light a smoke or roll a joint, we tripped the light fantastic for the remainder of the afternoon.

I've no idea how much time passed. It wasn't until I heard her familiar bellow from down below, "Carrie, what are you doing home from school?!" that I realized, we weren't in Kansas anymore. Thinking fast I called back, "I'm not feeling well. I'm sick." It took her only seconds to discover I wasn't alone. Mom watched a lot of cop shows. Plus, I made K leave his shoes at the door. She came back with, "Oh yeah?! Who are you "not feeling well" with?!" and then the whizbang of K's Doc Martins being launched and hitting the living room wall. Mom was a thrower, a thrower and a yeller when she was pissed. And she was often pissed. When pissed she cranked the volume and tore a verbal strip off whoever was the target. If the message was not received, or said target was frozen in fear, the projectiles started to fly. Luckily our pets and I were all quite agile. I looked at the bone-pale K and calmly suggested it was time we got dressed. He already had one leg in his jeans. I swam through the molasses river to where my kimono lay. The whole time my brain was split in two. Although one side was very aware of the clear and present danger known as Pissed Mom, the other side was thrilled to have fingers that looked like tentacles. "Get your ass down here!" "I'm just getting dressed, Mom." It came out sounding robustly happy, like I was ready to sing a jingle on the benefits of MDMA. Not good. It was time to kick into acting mode. Act afraid and guilty. That was my mantra, act afraid and guilty. All of my fuckus (focus + fuckedupedness = fuckus) was concentrated on becoming afraid. If I could just feel the fear, I would then have the appropriate reaction! I squeezed my eyes shut and thought of all things scary. It must have worked because when I finally opened my eyes the most terrifying thing happened. A fury of red curls and green eyes tore through the rice paper room divider. A mighty lioness ripped its way through the Asian jungle. I was both frightened and impressed. She had never looked so fierce, so strong. I'm guessing K had already slunk out of the room when my eyes were closed. It was just me and this amazing force of a woman, my mom. She yelled and yelled and yelled some more. I apologized profusely. Mom was the most important person in my life. Even in my drug induced state it hurt me deeply to know I'd disappointed her. Her punishment was to make me stay in my room for the remainder of the day and night with no dinner, no phone, no smokes and worst of all, no her. She didn't want to talk to me. Gutted, I rode out the rest of the trip alone, writing in my journal and attempting to put together the broken pieces of the room divider.

20

BADASSERY

I'M A GOOD PERSON who has done bad things. Aren't we all? To clarify, let's imagine bad behaviour on a spectrum; with gossip, swearing, and over-cooking steak on one end and life sentence hardcore crime on the other. I currently fall on the low end of the spectrum. Meaning that if I left a T-bone on the grill too long, I'd cuss like a motherfucker. As a teenager I dabbled in the mid-spectrum range. In no way am I proud of my criminal past but I'm banking on it being entertaining filler for this god-forsaken albatross, the memoir.

Shoplifting was a given. Everyone was doing it. Especially us West Mall types. I don't remember the first thing I stole but I do recall the thrill of getting away with it. That delicate dance of staying calm while your heart is clanging, moving slowly to not draw attention but being swift enough to slip your bounty into its hiding place in a pocket, up a sleeve or under a shirt without being seen. Lip gloss from Shoppers Drug Mart, cheese and pepperoni sticks from Safeway and earrings from Woolco were all easy targets. I must have been good at it too because I never got caught.

It was the summer of '85 and we were having a bush party in the letters that made up "Centennial Park." Apparently you could read "Centennial Park" from the sky. It was designed for all the travellers to see as they flew in and out of Pearson airport. Just like the Hollywood sign, except ours was made from manicured trees and there was no promise of celebrity sightings in the general vicinity.

That night started out like any other night with the usual suspects, my homeys, pouring down the coolies and super toking their way to oblivion and beyond. I was grooving to Kashmir on the ghetto blaster when suddenly an infiltrator strolls into the centre of the P. Who was this tall, scrawny, black-haired, blue-eyed, smiley stranger? He wasn't one of us. He looked like he had options. He brought a 2-4 and handed out smokes like they were business cards. I found out later that he fell in love with me that night. Something about the way I danced like everyone was watching.

He lived in a nice bungalow in Brampton with good, loving parents. For some reason he rebelled against them at every turn. I never understood why he was so hellbent for leather (Mom's expression, not mine) yet I found his recklessness irresistible and soon became the Bonnie to his Clyde. That summer was spent mating like feral animals, partying, and breaking into cars. We never smashed glass. That was for kids. Our targets were unlocked vehicles. Open windows were slightly more challenging but still less risky than shoplifting. There were no bright lights and eagle-eyed clerks to contend with. Every time you entered a car, there was the thrill of the unknown. What treasure would be lurking in a glove compartment? Would the cup holder have enough change in it for a pack of smokes? Maybe we'd find a bottle of vodka stashed under the driver seat. Certainly had my fair share of sunglasses that summer.

One night Clyde and I were coming back from my friend Penny's place in Mississauga. She had had a party and we were supposed to stay the night. Penny's mom had other plans. She kicked us out, which is why I was dragging a sleeping bag behind me. I was like that Peanuts' character with his blankie. What was his name?

Clyde and Bonnie drinking beers
at Mr. Greenjeans

It was very late. We were under-slept and over-served. We should have just gone to bed.

Look at that! Shiny silver cock-tease curves in the form of a 1975 Stingray convertible showing off in my parking lot. Sneering at us as if to say, check me out. Don't touch me. Just look and weep at what you can't have, will never have. What the fuck was this dick of a car doing at the corner of Bad and Ass?

No words were exchanged. The top was down. Open invite! We slipped in. I closed my eyes and sunk into the sumptuous leather, savouring every moment of borrowed luxury. I drifted deep into her delicious decadence and after some time purred, "Sleepy time. Let's go home." When I opened my eyes, I saw that Clyde had taken our penchant for petty theft to the next level.

"Yeah. Let's get the fuck outta here."

Waltzing into the house with a brand new Blaupunkt stereo was not an option. My bright idea was to wrap it in the sleeping bag and hide it between a chain link fence and a bush. The next day we would take it to a pawn shop. This was going to make us some decent coin. We slipped into the house without waking up Mom and passed out.

The next morning while tucking into a bowl of Shreddies, there was a loud knock at the door. Mom answered it. Two police officers entered. One was holding the stereo. The other was holding my sleeping bag. Turns out my name and address were written on the inside label, thanks to bloody Brownie camp. The police said someone had reported seeing a couple of teenagers breaking into vehicles the previous night. They asked me who I was with. Clyde ran up to the door and said it was all his idea, and that I was innocent. They handcuffed us both. I'll never forget the look on Mom's face as she watched me being led down the hallway to the waiting police car.

We were taken to the station, printed, processed and inter-rogated separately. I was shaking in my PJs. They offered me coffee. I asked for apple juice instead. I followed their instruc-tions and gave them a verbal and written account of the events. They encouraged me to place all the blame on Clyde because he was 18 with a handful of priors, and I was a 16-year-old honour student with a non-existent record. The fallout was: Clyde was fined $2,000 and put on probation while I was 'released with a warning' and ordered to refrain from all contact with my boyfriend.

On the way out of the station the officer who took our prints looked me in the eye and said, "Don't let me see you back here again, young lady."

"You won't." I replied. And I meant it. I wanted nothing more than to be at home with Mom, snuggling with the cats and watching cartoons. But first I needed a smoke. A smoke with Clyde. We had to say our goodbyes, right?

They let us light up right there inside the station. It was the '80s after all. In between drags, we necked with tragic urgency, kissing, smoking, and crying. The cops eventually had to break us up. Clyde and I went our separate ways.

Days later we picked up where we left off. We couldn't keep our hands off of each other or off of other people's stuff. My next arrest was for a theft under. Clyde was nailed for a hit and run. I broke up with him after that but still visited him in jail. We got back together briefly when he was released but then while high on acid he tried to outrun the police in a stolen vehicle. The trunk was filled with drugs. I imagine he went away for a long time. We've lost touch but I hope wherever he is now, he is clean, content, and living his best life.

21

JOE

ANYONE WHO SAYS HIGH SCHOOL was the time of their life is either a sociopath or went to Etobicoke School of the Arts. ESA was a haven for the gifted freaks and misfits.

Wannabe visual artists, musicians, actors, and dancers, honed their skills under the tutelage of seasoned professionals, all while maintaining a high academic standard. I believe 78.8% was the required grade point average. The colourful hallways were alive with song, dance, and perspiration.

On the first day of drama class, our teacher, Mr. Hislop, insisted we call him Joe.

He sat cross-legged on the floor while we gathered at his bare feet. Pushing stringy hair curtains behind his ears signalled that he was about to speak. His movements were deliberate and slow. His face like his clothes bore a lived-in fatigue. If he were to be subjected to sudden movement, it would not end well. Joe Hislop was a one-speed old wagon of a man. I clung to his every word.

JOE: If anyone is here because they want to be famous, leave right now. I'm not interested in teaching you. This is a drama program, not an acting for film and television course. If you want to be a star, walk out that door.

I want to be rich and famous. Doesn't everyone?! Is that not why we are here, in this faux FAME school? This place is modelled after a fucking TV show! I scanned the room. No one even glanced at the exit sign.

JOE: Everything you learn in this room with me is designed to prepare you for the stage. Theatre, the most ancient form of storytelling, is not merely entertainment; it holds the mirror up to society. As players it is your job to be the reflection. It's not enough to put on a funny hat and accent. That might get you a commercial gig but after you spend your sweet residual cheque on more funny hats and cocaine, it's back to flipping burgers, waiting for your agent to call. In this class you will learn what it takes to embody a role. You will dig deep, uncover, lay bare what you are truly made of. You will mine the shit out of yourself. Great acting begins from within. I am here, to guide you, to help you, to go inside you.

Whoa. What?

Wait.

While those were not his exact words, Joe Hislop did have a handful (pun intended) of inappropriate relationships with students during his time at ESA. Years after our graduating class, enough complaints were made that he was removed from teaching duties and stashed away in an office to serve out his remaining days far from his unsuspecting prey.

I was never one of his victims. This strikes me as miraculous, seeing as so many other adult males treated me like fair game. I liked Joe. I even trusted him enough to share some problems I was having at home.

We met in the supply room off of the black box theatre.

ME: I'm having problems at home. (starting to well up.)
JOE: (lighting our smokes.) Oh? Why? What's going on?
ME: I'm hanging with the wrong crowd, partying a lot, drinking and doing drugs.

JOE: Typical, 'After School Special' stuff. Smiling sadly under heavy-hooded eyes

ME: Our place is party central. Mom's like if you're gonna drink and do drugs you may as well do 'em here, where you're not gonna get caught.

JOE: What kind of drugs are you doing?

ME: Mostly pot and hash, a little acid and shrooms

JOE: Just soft drugs then. You're not doing coke?

ME: Not with my mom.

JOE: That's good. You can't become addicted to pot and hash.

ME: I just hate my life. Everyone here is like rich and like nice and I'm just like this fucked up stoner.

JOE: The staff here are aware of your situation. They know where you're from. It's true. You're not like the other kids here. Don't worry about fitting in with them. Be yourself.

In hindsight I understand how his advice was meant to be comforting but, at that moment, 16-year-old Carrie needed to hear, "Poor child. You deserve much better than this hand you've been dealt. I will find you a new place to live with responsible adults and a pool."

Maybe I shouldn't have omitted all the ugly details, like Mom's boyfriend Mitch punching me in the face. Joe may have been more proactive if he knew I didn't always feel safe in my own home. Like on school nights when Mitch skulked in uninvited, I fled to Naomi's place. She was always in the basement working on an impossibly intricate drawing, while her brother practiced classical piano up above on the main floor. Kay, her gentle sad mom, was usually taking a bath. Their house smelled of rice, ginger, and damp newspaper. I was grateful for this sanctuary. And Naomi was very welcoming...at first. But the deeper I got in with The West Mall crew, the more we grew apart. Naomi didn't approve of my friends from 'The Hood.' She was disappointed in me. Hell. So was I. I wore my shame like an impenetrable leather jacket.

It's no surprise our friendship did not survive high school. By the time we were 18, I had already been stripping for a year. Naomi was weighing out her scholarships for post secondary options. My dad was...? Who the hell knows where. He had pulled yet another disappearing act. Needless to say the sex pact he had with my friend was made null and void. Thank God for small miracles.

22

CHANTELL MY HELL

W E WERE BOTH 16 when we started to hang out. I was just as attracted to her as I was afraid of her. Chantell Naveau was half Mohawk and half French Canadian. She was all sharp angles and dangerous curves with the most exquisite face I'd ever seen. Her voice was deep. She spoke quickly and quietly. I spent a lot of time asking her to repeat herself. Sorry, what did you say? Sorry. She was always at least one step ahead of me. And I was always apologizing.

CHANTELL: Come to KFC with me.
ME: Sorry. I don't have any money.
CHANTELL: Check your cowshit coochkins.
ME: Sorry. What did you say?
CHANTELL: I found six bucks in my couch cushions.
ME: Score!
CHANTELL: Don't get too excited. The chicken's for my little sister. Fucking Mom disappeared again.
ME: Harsh. I don't need to eat. Let's go to KFC.

I would have followed her to hell and back or worse, Scarborough.

Maybe some of her exotic hotness would rub off on me.

Since reading Jim Morrison's, "No One Here Gets Out Alive," I wanted to be Indigenous so bad. I dyed my hair blue black, made some feather earrings and resurrected Mom's suede fringed vest. She stopped wearing it in '73. It had a blood stain on it from when Dad punched her so hard he left a permanent scar through her left eyebrow.

Chantell was not offended by my fashion choice. Her personal look was heavy metal slut witch. Everything she wore was tight, trashy and deadly. Her room was covered in posters of bands I'd never heard of and she had dolls strung up by the neck, hanging from her ceiling. She was interested in witchcraft and was obsessed with buying a book of spells.

CHANTELL: It's really expensive, you'll have to pish in. We need to bury it in a cemetery and only take it out under a full moon to do our spells.

Whenever she talked scary shit I heard her clear as a bell.

CHANTELL: School's Out's playing at Gas Works tonight. Let's drop acid and go.

The last time we did acid together was at a toga party. She looked like a heavy metal slut witch meets Grecian Goddess. I looked like someone wrapped in a bed sheet. Of course Anthony—my boyfriend at the time—had the hots for her. They hooked up after I passed out in the guest bedroom. It was a messed up night. I returned home in a different sheet than the one I wore when I left. Even though Chantell stole my guy, I was too afraid of her to get angry. In fact, I apologized.

Sorry, I passed out.

Sorry, I left you alone with Anthony.

Sorry, he was uncircumcised.

Gross, eh?

Sorry.

Off we went to Gasworks to see the Alice Cooper cover band, School's Out.

Gasworks was a notorious hang out for bikers, strippers and minors. In the '80s every ozone-destroying hair band played there or wanted to. I saw Helix, Anvil, Jump (Van Halen Tribute band) and Highway to Hell (AC/DC cover band) all before my eighteenth birthday. I don't actually recall much about the band on this particular night. There may have been a boa constrictor winding its way up our Alice clone but what held my attention more was watching Chantell cast a spell on her prey. She zeroed in on a tall, long-haired cutie with good teeth. Let's call him Steve. Steve bought us beer and, at first, I was convinced he liked me. It wasn't until the three of us went back to his place I realized how wrong I was. Chantell and Steve told me to stay in the living room while they slipped away upstairs. They hissed at me to keep the lights off.

STEVE: My mom will freak out if you wake her up.
CHANTELL: Don fukz this up Sarrie!

I sat there on a strange couch in the dark, as still as can be for I don't know how long.

Acid bends time, space, and one's brain. The first tip-toed attempt at retracing my steps back to the front door, led to a closet. I would have laughed if I wasn't already feeling sorry for myself. Eventually I found the exit and started walking. Where the fuck am I? I've got to find a subway station. As long as I find a subway station, I can make my way home. Keep walking. Walk faster. Why didn't I pay attention when we left Gasworks? It was a long walk to Steve's place. Wasn't it? Just keep on walking. At least I'm not tired. I am too high to feel sleepy. On I walk. Walk walk walk towards the light. Ah-hah! There it is—the Christie Subway Station! I march up to the doors, hope restored and...it is closed. What time is it?

I had to know the time. The streets were dead. I walked not half a block and pushed open the next door I saw. Comforting smells of old wood and sour cabbage hit me upside the head and drew me up a flight of stairs. There was a series of open doors to the left and right. I poked my nose in each one, looking for a clock. There it was, a perfunctory circle with imposing arms suggesting it was way past my bedtime, yet hours before the subway would start up. A taxi home was my only option. I would need money for that. There must be something in this room worth $30. From the giant table, calendar, whiteboards and blackboards, I knew I had stumbled upon a meeting place of great importance. The energy was heavy. The clock was ticking—literally and loudly too. The pressure was on. I darted about. Looking up, looking down, opening and closing drawers and then ... my heart stopped at the beauty before me. Perched on top of a filing cabinet in all her shiny metallic bad assiest glory sat the biggest ghetto blaster I had ever seen. She was also the heaviest thing I had ever lifted. Carrying her down the stairs was an Olympic event but giving up wasn't an option. This thing would get me a ride all the way to Niagara Falls!

I didn't have to flag the first taxi I saw.

He rolled alongside me as I limped my way up the sidewalk.

TD (taxi driver): Need a lift?
ME: What does it look like?
His car smelled like old ball caps and fake pine trees.
It was warm. He asked what I was doing at The Korean Cultural Club at four o'clock in the morning.
I had to pee. The door was open so ... He let that go and then started drilling me about the boombox.

TD: Why are you dragging that thing around?

ME: I brought it to my buddy's party.

TD: You can barely lift it.

ME: Good thing you came around when you did!

TD: Where did you get it?

ME: What?

TD: The Sony Sound System with it's own zip code.

ME: It was a gift from my boyfriend.

TD: Did you leave him at the party?

ME: Who?

TD: Your boyfriend?

ME: What? No. He's in jail.

TD: For what?

ME: Two counts of theft over, possession with intent, and hit and run.

TD: Sounds like a keeper.

ME: More like a lifer.

And then we laughed. He said I was funny and asked if I felt like having a beer on his boat.

You can't make this shit up.

His boat was parked along the lakeshore in Mimico. We went 'down below' and got to know one another. Not in the biblical sense. Miraculously nothing sexual happened. He was too beige and practical for my tastes. He was a nice guy too. Definitely not my type. I told him how old I was and he lectured me about the dangers of being out late and alone. I pretended to agree with him because, beer. The beer helped dull the clanging rattle left behind by the LSD's departure.

By the time he drove me home it was full daylight and I was ready to sleep.

Yet there was one more challenge before bedtime.

I was locked out. Again.

Mom was MIA. Again.

I placed the ghetto blaster behind the screen door and jumped down into the window well. The small glass pane popped out easily leaving just enough room for my anorexic body to squeeze through. I ran up the stairs, opened the door and retrieved my beautiful boombox.

I was proud of my giant haul. It was the biggest thing I had ever lifted. I dragged it up to my room and played with all the dials and buttons. There was a cassette still in the dock. I pressed play and laid down on my bed.

"Chobojaleul wihan hoehwajeog yeong-eo sogae—An introduction to conversational English for beginners."

This instructional tape was oddly soothing. I let it lull me to sleep every night for a week until I finally sold the Sony for $75 to a kid who wanted to be a breakdancer.

I sincerely apologize to the Korean Community Centre at Christie and Bloor. Sorry for stealing your portable stereo. I hope I didn't hinder your ability to learn conversational English.

For what it's worth your stereo went to a good home and helped a young man realize his dreams.

23

SLEEP MY
ELUSIVE FRIEND

M Y BOYFRIEND CLYDE was a regular at our place. Mom liked him. He was a nonviolent happy drunk. A rarity in our neighborhood. He slept over often but wasn't allowed to spend the night in my room. That didn't stop me from trying to sneak him in whenever I could but on nights when Mom was home and sober he slept on the living room couch.

One particularly boozy night we stumbled in and went straight to our respective beds. Mom had passed out earlier and Mitch was still awake, in his chair, listening to the band Yes on the headphones.

I fell asleep immediately. Some time later I'm awakened by a hand on my breast. I shake my shoulder and make a pissed-off sound to let Clyde know I'm not interested. That's not like him to bug me in my sleep. The hand disappears and I drift off again. Moments later there's a dick prodding at me from behind.

A lightning bolt of white fear jolts me upright. I turn to see him lying there and I take off down the stairs yelling, "Wake up! Wake up! Mitch just tried to fuck me! Mom?! Get up, call the cops! Get this fucking asshole out of here!!!"

I've made it to the couch. Clyde gazelles up the stairs, three at a time. I hug my knees in tight and start to rock back and forth. Clyde is threatening to kill Mitch, Mom screams for Mitch to get the fuck out of her house and never come back.

I freeze.

All of the important parts of me exit the building.

From this safe distance I recall the last time I heard those words, "never come back." It was a year ago, after he had punched me in the face and pinned us both against the wall with our kitchen table. The cops came and a peace bond was issued. We were blissfully Mitch-free for a few months. I also recalled the last time a dick tried to push its way in without my permission.

On that occasion my mouth was the chosen hole.

I was a child.

The dick belonged to my mom's dad.

The front door slams shut. The finality of that sound brings me back. Mom is on my left and Clyde is on my right, offering me smokes and a bottle of Blue. I don't want either. I just want to stay awake forever.

24

HOW DID
YOU GET INTO IT?

'Uncle Lou's—Waitress for hire.
No experience necessary. Apply in person today.'

The address was somewhere in the bowels of North York, close to where my mom's new boyfriend lived. Maybe I'd pop in for a visit and see if she had some cash to lend me. I hadn't seen her in days and I had nothing beyond bus fare. I really needed this job.

I raided Mom's closet for a matching red shirt and skirt combo with black kitten heels. I looked mature, competent, and hireable.

I set out to the corner of West Mall and Rathburn and waited for the bus.

It was a hot summer day. The kind of day you just want to grab a case of beer and sit in the park. I'm counting my change when this big white convertible pulls up.

GUY in CAR: Hey! You need a ride somewhere?
ME: Mom always told me not to take rides from strangers.
GUY in CAR: She's a smart woman.
ME: You obviously haven't met her.

I'd always wanted to ride in a topless car. Marco drove me to Uncle Lou's. I wrote up a resumé on the back of a paper place mat while we drank Harvey Wallbangers. Up to that point I had worked at McDonald's and Yogen Früz and was fired from both. I got caught stealing giant cans of red sockeye from Yogen Früz. No. They didn't make salmon-flavoured yogurt. As well as dessert, the mall kiosks offered sandwiches too. One of my tasks was to make said sandwiches. Every time I made a salmon sandwich I thought of Mom back home opening up another tin of sadness (flakes o' ham) and I felt sorry for her. She deserved a little sockeye in her life. McDonald's let me go because I failed their speed test. Once a month they would time how long it took to complete an order; from punching it in on the cash register, retrieving the food items, and assembling the bag. The weekend before the speed test, The Insiders (my girl gang) and I had discovered the joys of Dexatrim. Dexatrim was a popular diet pill of the eighties. It was easily pockcted from the shelves of Shoppers Drug Mart and contained a heart-pounding wallop of chemicals that suppress your appetite for food and sleep. I popped a handful before my shift. Halfway through the day, the manager appeared with a stopwatch. Quarter Pounder with cheese, large fries, small orange drink, and an apple turnover. Big Mac, small fries, chocolate shake, chicken nuggets, two honey mustard dips, large coke, hot fudge sundae, three happy meals, one burger two cheeseburgers three sprite three large fries two quarterpoundersbigmacholdthemayovanillamilkshake...

MANAGER: STOP!
He clicks off the stopwatch.
MANAGER: Schiffler, meet me in the staffroom.
He indicates for me to sit. Sitting felt wrong. There were orders to fill. Hungry people to feed!
MANAGER: I want to discuss the results of your speed test.

ME: Did I pass?

MANAGER: Never in my entire career as McDonald's manager have I seen results like these. Granted this is a fast food restaurant but the kitchen was doing their darndest and they just could not keep up with you!"

My feet were tap dancing. Was he done? I had work to see and people to do.

Please enjoy one last complementary filet-o-fish and leave your uniform in the laundry bin.

I did not mention the details of my termination to Uncle Lou.

I could barely get a word in with motor-mouth Marco.

MARCO: I do construction, framing, drywall—you name it. Used to DJ. Worked at Caddy's, y'know, the strip club? You remind me of a girl there, a good girl. Pretty and smart, like you.

ME: I've thought of danc…

MARCO: How's the Wallbanger? You like the Wallbanger?

ME: I…

MARCO: Lou, bring us another round. I like how you chew the straw. You're very watchable. Star quality. You got Vegas written all over you.

Marco kept saying nice things to me. And shit, vodka in a greasy spoon is almost as good as beer in a park. That night we ended up in the basement of his dad's barbershop. He was short, hairy and uncircumcised. The next day he took me to the Million Dollar Saloon.

I didn't know where to look or not look. It was a riot of neon, chrome, smoke, and music so loud it sent my heart pinballing around the room. Beautiful women in various states of undress slunk and strutted along the two stages. One was having a shower in a plexiglass box suspended from the ceiling. It was an adults-only amusement park and I wanted an all-access pass.

I had to get on one of those stages. Marco primed me for what to say.

We yelled at each other over the music.

MARCO: YOU REMEMBER WHAT TO SAY TO SAM?
ME: SAM? SAM WHO?
MARCO: SAM. THE MANAGER SAM!
ME: RIGHT RIGHT RIGHT—OF COURSE I DO!
MARCO: HE'S GONNA ASK HOW OLD ARE YOU!
ME: NINETEEN. I AM 19.
MARCO: WHERE'S YOUR BURLESQUE ENTERTAINERS' LICENCE?
ME: I LEFT IT IN WINDSOR.
MARCO: WHAT CLUB?
ME: PLATINUM HOUSE.
MARCO: GOOD GIRL!

It was that easy. I talked to Sam for like two minutes. He pointed to the change room and told me I was up next.

I didn't have anything to change into. I was still wearing Mom's red cotton number. That would have to be what I 'opened with.' My bra and underwear were nothing fancy. In fact they didn't even match. Good thing I wouldn't be keeping them on for long! I brushed my hair, applied more lipstick and went to the DJ booth as instructed. He told me I would be on Stage two. Stage Two girls dance to whatever music the Stage One girl picks. Fine by me. "What's your stage name?"

Stage name??? Marco skipped that part.

Ahhhhhh—CAT!

Note to self: Choo Choo and Schultz's food dish would need to be filled when I got home.

DJ: Gentlemen, let's make some noise for Miss T Nights on Stage One and on Stage Two…rub your hairy palms together for Caa-aat!!!

I burst into a flurry of all the moves I learned from the three years of dance classes at The Etobicoke School of the Arts. I step ball chained grand jaunteed grapevined jazz handed my way out of my clothes until I was naked as the day I was born. Now what? I watched the girl on Stage One for clues. She was on her hands and knees, crawling like a panther one minute and then humping the floor the next. I copied her as best I could. The whole time I could not wipe the big goofy grin off my face. This was fun with a capital EFF U! When the music was over I blew kisses to my bemused audience, bowed and threw my clothes back on before meeting up with Sam for the verdict. He was sure to hire me.

SAM: How old did you say you were?
ME: (surfing the adrenaline high) I am 19!
SAM: Right.
ME: Why? What's wrong?
SAM: Get your licence, shave yourself and come back in a couple of birthdays.

I ran out of there to look for Marco. It took me a while to find his car. He had put the roof back on the convertible. I didn't recognize it right away. He was different too. Quiet.
ME: Hey! Did you see that? What did you think?
(Pause)
MARCO: I didn't see it all.
ME: What did you think of the part you did see?
(Longer pause)

MARCO: Not much.
ME: (Starting to cry.) I wanna go home.
MARCO: You're just...too young or...something.
ME: TAKE ME HOME—NOW!!!

I didn't want to see his gross dick again anyway. But I definitely was not done with stripping. Those twelve minutes on stage were the most exciting twelve minutes of my life. Maybe I wasn't that good but I believed that with practice I could be great! Stripping was my destiny. After feeding the cats, I called every place in the yellow pages until I found one that didn't have an age requirement. 'The Tramp' was in a dingy basement on Main Street in east Toronto. I felt much more at home there than I did at The Million Dollar Saloon. Mind you, the bikers freaked me out. Every day at four o'clock the Paradise Riders lumbered down the stairs and stuffed the small space with leather and fear. I avoided eye contact and prayed they would never ask me to table dance. They didn't. Even stranger than their complete disinterest in me was what they drank. Upon their arrival, pitchers of milk and several small beer glasses were set in front of them with an efficiency reserved for esteemed guests. They drank their milk and barely said a word. Silence makes no mistakes? Aside from these tense daily visits, The Tramp was a good place for me to hone some skills. I learned how to get the clientele to stay for just one more drink, and always at least one more table dance.

25

DEAR DIARY

SOME MIGHT SAY I was good at keeping secrets. Others might say I was one sneaky son of a bitch. Either way I kept my new profession from the parental units for months. I came and went as I pleased. Neither of them was home enough to even notice the late hours I was keeping. Splitting my time between our place on The West Mall and Dad's apartment on Queen East was super convenient. I had somewhere to hang my tassels at both ends of the city! That first summer of stripping was a circus of men, money, sweat, and smoke.

I didn't stay at The Tramp for long. It was a convenient place to learn the ropes but I quickly outgrew its little stage and thin crowd of regulars. Joan of Dark—receptionist by day, stripper by night—told me I was meant for better places. She talked one of her office co-workers (Shelly BleepBleep) into lending me her ID.

I took her ID, to the federal licencing borough, handed over 80 bucks in five-dollar bills and voila! I, Shelly BleepBleep, born in 1967, was a fully licenced Burlesque Entertainer. I could flash this new photo ID in a bouncer's face and pretty much work in whatever club I wanted.

And I did.

My stage name was Tabitha. I'm a Bewitched fan. If I don't need to explain what that means—congratulations! You too have great taste in 1970's sitcoms.

That summer Tabitha cast a spell on all the iconic stages of downtown Toronto: Zanzibar, Brass Rail, French Maid, House of Lancaster, and of course Filmore's. I gave a hundred percent every time.

My shows were fast-paced and athletic. More dancey than trancey. I was only 17, with energy to burn. It wasn't enough for me to strut across the stage, bend over, pose, repeat. I had to *dance*. Every move I ever learned at the Etobicoke School of the Arts was mashed together into three songs of semi-sexy weirdness. I was a hot mess. One club owner said, "Not everyone wants to see you jumping around like a monkey."

While the stage may have been my experimental playground, I was all business on the floor.

Table dances were where the money was at.

For five bucks a song, we danced naked on little wooden cubes that were wedged between the feet of strangers.

The trick was to get as close as you could without touching. Let them see it all up close and very personal. If a customer got caught even thinking about grabbing a handful, they were thrown out. The bouncers looked out for us. I felt much safer on the floor than I did in the changeroom.

The changerooms didn't vary much from club to club. No matter the size, they were never big enough to accommodate our hair, heels, and egos. They were overcrowded toxic tombs. A fog of hairspray, cigarettes, and lady funk hovered beneath the fluorescent lights. There's Blondie clipping her toenails. On the counter next to her foot, a line of coke is hoovered by Mimi who finally kicked out her dealer boyfriend for good dis time. Roxette has been working doubles all week. She's asleep on the floor under an oversized fox fur coat. On the only other chair, Mercedes is perched with a Singapore Sling in one hand and a mascara wand in the other. She can't stop crying long enough to put her makeup on. All around me are women in various states of undress shouting over one another. Fuck they scared me. I avoided them and the changeroom as much as possible.

No problem. I was there to make money, not friends. Guu-uuurrrrl, I made some money! For the first time in my life I was raking it in, and I was hooked.

By the time school started up in September, I reluctantly switched to working weekends only. The folks still bought the story that I was waitressing at a high-end bistro. I also moved all my stuff over to Dad's place. He had a new girlfriend and was the happiest I'd ever seen him. Lesley was a poli-sci student. She wore glasses, corduroys, and no makeup. She brought out the well-read wannabe academic in my father and he helped her get in touch with her more...uh... primitive nature. She lived only two blocks away. They spent most of their evenings together at her place. Once again I was left to my own devices. I was only 17. My 'devices' were not even fully formed! Did they really think I was going to stay at home every night and study? Didn't they know that when the cat's away the mice will go to a pub and bring home a random? On one such night, big Daddy Cat came back just in time to catch me playing with my new toy.

Dad freaked out. "It's a school night," blah blah blah, "not under my roof! You're only sixteen for Christ's sake. And who the fuck is this asshole?! Get the fuck outta my house! Come near my daughter again and I'll fucking kill

'Dad and Leslie.' Handsome dude who
started losing his teeth later that same year.

you!!! She's only 16!" and "What the fuck are you doing with
your life, Carrie?! Use your fucking brain!!!"

I swear my internal organs shut down. This is what slow
death felt like.

Dad had never yelled at me before. Oh, he was a belliger-
ent, mean, and violent drunk, but I was never the target of his
cruelty. Up until that night I could do no wrong.

I'm 17, Dad.

He wouldn't even look at me. He couldn't. He stormed off
to his room and slammed the door.

I started packing.

THE LAST TIME I'D BEEN TO NIAGARA FALLS was when I was a kid. I loved how the mist made me feel so clean and how the neon lights of the busy downtown made me feel so... dirty? Niagara Falls was an exciting adults-only mystery.

The following is so cringy I just have to share it.

It's an excerpt from my journal. I wrote it the next morning while waiting for the train to Niagara Falls. A lost bird had just flown out of Union Station but not before much flailing.

> *October 9, 1986*
> *I started to feel panicky when my little friend was*
> *flying around and banging its head against the*
> *walls. I know the desperation those closest to me will*
> *feel when they'll be unable to catch me but none-*
> *theless I must fly. I don't like having my two feet on*
> *the ground anymore. I hope no one catches up with*
> *me for a good long while. This is my adventure; no*
> *matter what the outcome will be I have to go out*
> *and live for myself only.*

Sweet Jeezus.

I met two memorable characters on the train. Charlotte was a hard-livin' 28-year-old. Her skin was a mess and her voice sounded like she gargled with bleach and broken glass. She was gonna quit stripping once she had enough money saved to get her daughter back.

Max was a German tourist. His plan was to see the Falls and then hitchhike to New York.

Charlotte took it upon herself to be a tour guide. She told us where to eat and what places to avoid. She introduced us to her friends at Lilly's Cafe, found us a motel for only $20 a night and then—poof—she disappeared into the mist.

Like me, Max was also on a budget. It made good sense for us to share a room.

Upon Charlotte's recommendation we had Chinese at The Golden Phoenix and then did the long walk to the Falls. For your reading pleasure, here is another excerpt from my 1986 journal.

> *I have visited them many times in the past but never have I wondered at their natural beauty with such awe as I did last night. It could be that my age has taught me to appreciate more but I prefer to think romantically and so I hold Max's exotic company responsible for those feelings. I'd like so much to go to New York with him but I'm sure I would suffer later by taking that impulsive action. I have to think of school, my family and friends. I'm sure they are all panicking now as it is. Yet. Here sits my ticket to New York and with a handsome, intelligent man at that!*

Oh, my misspent youth. I should have been writing for Hallmark! Although, sex with Max was anything but romantic.

It was cool and efficient, very … German.

The next morning he pulled out a metal tool from his toiletry bag and handed it to me. "It's for your pits." It was a pimple extractor. He showed me how to use it on my chin.

That was a mood killer, but I still wept as I watched him walk towards the Canadian/US border. In his long leather coat and practical boots, he marched on to the land of opportunities without once glancing back.

Finally alone, I was free to get to work. The Concord was nothing fancy but the staff were welcoming and the other dancers were actually friendly. Again because I was young and healthy (no visible addictions) I made a killing. I worked there for a few nights before the cash started to burn a hole in my jeans. Wouldn't it be fun to go shopping in Buffalo?! If Max could hitchhike to the States, surely taking a taxi would be even easier.

I was asked to step out of the cab and into their cubicle.

BORDER PATROL #1: We need to ask you some questions.
BORDER PATROL #2: Just routine.
BORDER PATROL #3: What's your name?
ME: Shelly.
BP #1: Last name?
ME: Sorry. Shelly BleepBleep.
BP #2: What is the purpose of your visit?
ME: Purpose?
BP #3: Business or pleasure?
ME: Neither. I just want to go shopping.
BP #1: How much money are you taking with you into the States?
ME: Ummm $200?
BP #2: How old are you, Shelly BleepBleep?
ME: Nineteen.
BP #1: Hand over your purse, please.
BP #3: We need to see the contents of your purse.

I hand over my calfskin fringed bag. They point to a wooden bench. I sit down and watch as they disappear into a room closing the door behind them.

They didn't seem to care that I had a taxi meter running.

Finally after what felt like an eternity they returned. BP#1 was holding my journal open, head down, lips moving. He was reading my fucking journal! BP#2 was stuffing my various IDs back into the wallet and BP#3 had my purse in one hand and a sock in the other. Shit. I hadn't bothered to unfold the fives and stick them in my wallet. I just balled them up and shoved them in a sock. Bloody amateur.

They set my belongings down on the counter and indicated to me to put everything back in its place.

BP #1: So, Shelly Bleep Bleep—or should we call you Carrie Schiffler?

ME: Um, Carrie is…

BP #3: We get it. There's dancers coming across here all the time.

BP #2: We got no problem with that.

BP #3: But we're not letting you across today, miss.

BP #1: Do yourself a favour and call your Dad.

BP #2: He's probably worried sick.

BP #3: Let him know you're okay.

BP #1: Better yet—just go home.

The taxi driver didn't bat an eye when I told him to drop me off back at the Concord. It was a good pay day for him. I on the other hand felt ripped off and violated. They read my fucking journal! My skin was crawling. I wrote down E-V-E-R-Y-T-H-I-N-G back then. Those border buffoons broke into my secret world. They helped themselves to a platter full of my private thoughts, confessions, and dreams. I felt sick to my stomach. I just wanted to go home. FUCK! Fuckin' fuckers. Maybe they were right.

I got on the next train back to Toronto.

Here's another journal entry written that day.

October 16, 1986

I'm on my way home. It's hard to believe. I was soooo tempted to stay and live my own life, to travel across Canada, and eventually Europe would be easy considering the money I can make in seven hours. It seems so inviting but until I see one dancer who is truly fulfilled and happy I don't dare risk all. Going to school tomorrow is such a scary thought. How much have I missed? In this competitive field an actor cannot afford to miss a day let alone three. Now my self opinion and my peers' suspicions will put me at the bottom step of my ladder to success.

I wonder if Dad told Mom I ran away. I'm going to have some serious explaining to do. Yet I don't know what I should say. That will be my Academy Award-winning improv. This humour is only to mask my fear. How is it possible for someone to be so strong and yet so scared?

I had a flair for the dramatic. I'll give myself that.

When I got home Dad was waiting for me. He was sprawled on the living room floor in his shorts with a two-litre bottle of Canadian cooler, two cups, an ashtray, and a pack of smokes.

I put my suitcase in my room and joined him on the floor. He passed me a cup and a lit smoke.

I spilled my guts, confessed my sins, apologized and delivered it all on a wave of tears.

DAD: I knew it. I figured that's what you were up to. Remember that dance you did for me and Evie? That was good. You were a natural, haha! No shame in that. You should have told me up front though. I don't like liars. I like peelers though. You making good money?

ME: (nodding)

DAD: Great. Now you can help pay some bills around here.

And I did. We agreed that I would give him half the rent money.

It was only fair I shared the wealth with Mom, too. I treated her to some fine dining and took her to see Pink Floyd, and Cats. We always had a good time together as long as I didn't start talking about work. She wanted to remain blissfully ignorant. And I didn't want to upset her. She was quite content at the time. Her new boyfriend, Dave, was the first older man she had ever taken up with. He was also the first boyfriend to not hit her.

MOM: He's too old to land a punch!

26

ROBINS EGGS

I VOWED TO STAY AWAY FROM COKE. I had smoked and snorted it only a handful of times when I was sixteen. It wasn't easy to come by at the corner of Bad and Ass. No one could afford it.

But, as you know, strippers and blow go together like … well, strippers and blow.

I'm proud to say I turned down all offers and never once used it during my three years as a dancer. I'm not so proud to say I stole a large bag of Robins Eggs I found in Dave's house, and womped through them in under a month.

Robins Eggs—37.5 mg of Phentermine, methyl-amphet-amine.

Named Robins Eggs for their white and blue speckled appearance. Other street names: Phen Fen, Uppers, Bennies.

It was and still is a prescription drug used for weight loss in obese people. It is an energy-giving mood enhancer that suppresses appetite and leaves one feeling full. But wait. There's more!!

Why settle for an oral dose when you can crush and snort or crush and smoke!

You too can rule the world, stay up all night and wake up on a beach in Acapulco, emaciated and ready to die.

Meanwhile on the homefront…

Leslie broke up with Dad—something about needing to focus on her studies. This kicked him into deep depression mode. He disappeared into his books, smokes, and Canada

Coolers. Rather than walk the 15 feet to the bathroom he peed in empty booze bottles, which also served as ashtrays.

My boyfriend Shayne told his folks about the deplorable conditions of my home life. They took pity on me and plans were in motion for me to move in. They were lovely people with a nice bungalow in Scarborough.

I was really struggling at school too. I was barely staying afloat but the heads of the drama department threw me a lifeline. They gave me the role of Jocasta in the grade 12 mainstage production of Oedipus The King. My peers were just as shocked as I was. We all thought Angela Hunter was poised for the female lead. She was talented, hard working and unlike me, she showed up to class.

I was handed the gifts of a stable home, a coveted role, and a relationship with a good kid who actually loved me— and what do I do? Go on a bender with stolen drugs.

In the weeks leading up to opening night of Oedipus, I covered a lot of terrain. That's what speed will do to a person. I was everywhere except for at rehearsals. I moved my stuff into Shayne's place but didn't sleep there much, because a) I wasn't sleeping, b) I didn't like Shayne as much as he liked me, and c) I wasn't sleeping.

I killed time and brain cells at the Gasworks and even ran into Chantell there where we did rails of my magic speckled powder in the bathroom.

I returned to the corner of Bad and Ass to share my stash with the homies and show off my rabbit fur. I worked all the clubs in Toronto and Niagara Falls and yet through this drug-induced mania I still somehow dragged my scrawny ass back to school two days before opening night. No one was more disappointed to see me than my understudy, Angela.

I told everyone I had been sick with strep throat. It wasn't a hard sell. My throat was fucked and I sounded like I ate sandpaper for breakfast. "Don't worry I've been working on the script," I croaked.

The director, Mr. Kramer, fell for it. The show must go on!

Just like me, the show came and went. I'll spare you the gory details because I blocked most of them out but rest assured I put the JOKE back in JOCasta. I was dead awful. In the final scene where the Queen stabs her own eyes out I swear I heard the audience whisper, *Just do it, for the love of god, please do it.* I sucked so bad there was no way I could ever show my strung-out face at ESA again. The next day I booked a two-week trip to Mexico.

27

STRANGER TRIP

I've always loved flying, especially back in the eighties when my ass was smaller and the seats were larger. Back then you could smoke on commercial flights too. I had just lit up a DuMaurier Ultra Light King Size to enjoy with a tomato juice when Karen, my travel companion, asked, "What type of dance do you do?"

Was she being serious right now?

Hadn't Georgina (our travel agent) told her where I worked?

Karen and I were partnered up by Georgina from the Niagara Falls Travel agency.

I was fine travelling solo. In fact I preferred it. I needed to clear my head and detox the phentermine out of my system and I wanted to do it alone.

Georgina was very insistent I travel with a buddy. Not only was it safer but I'd save a lot of money too. She knew just the buddy.

Karen was a waitress at a well-known surf-and-turf up the road. Like me, she was also looking to get away somewhere warm and affordable. Unlike me, she didn't want to travel alone. Georgina set up a meeting to see if Karen and I were compatible. We met at Karen's restaurant. I had been there a few times before. In fact the service was so slow it made dining-and-dashing a no brainer. Thankfully none of the staff recognized me. Georgina introduced us. Carrie, this is Karen. Karen, this is Carrie, she's a dancer. I looked Karen in the eye, smiled and asked her if she was okay with that. For sure! she chirped. We laughed, made small talk, signed the papers and here we are a week later jetting off to Mexico together!

ME: Sorry?
KAREN: What type of dance do you do Jazz, ballet, modern…?

Before answering her, I take a big gulp of juice and regret not ordering a Bloody Mary.

ME: I'm a stripper. Thought I'd mentioned that at the restaurant?

Karen blinks, turns her head to stare out the window and blinks some more.

KAREN: How old did you say you were?
ME: Just turned 18.
KAREN: Well we're gonna need some house rules.

The revelation that she was saddled with a teenage stripper was a game changer. Karen took it upon herself to play chaperone. Convinced I was bad news, she would not allow me out of her sight. She insisted on following me everywhere—to the pool, the buffet line, to the beach. She was always inches away, breathing down my neck, waiting for me to what—throw my bikini into the ocean, shoot heroin and give blowjobs to the bar staff?

I kept reassuring her I wasn't there to party and I really just needed some R-n-R. I omitted the bit about the recent bennie binge, murdering Oedipus, and dropping out of school. Why throw fuel at her fear?

We were a good five days into our stay when Karen finally started to show her true colours.

KAREN: See those two guys over there?

I lifted my head off the towel and looked to where she was pointing.

ME: What about them?

KAREN: Rob is from Ohio and Julio is from here.

ME: And?

KAREN: Aren't they cute?

ME: (I look again. They wave this time.) They're okay.

KAREN: They want to take us out for dinner.

ME: Not interested.

KAREN: Why not?

ME: House rule #1: no hooking up. Remember?

KAREN: It's just dinner.

ME: It's never just dinner.

KAREN: C'mon, they're super nice and Julio can show us around town. We have to mingle with the locals. It's the only way to get to know a country.

I conceded but only because I was already bored with the food at the resort.

We arrived at Playa Taco at the designated time. Karen was dressed to impress and had put a little extra shimmer on her face. She was short and curvy, pretty in a wholesome kind of way. With her waist-length hair she definitely could turn some heads. But when she spoke, people turned their heads alright—turned to look for an exit sign. She was tightly wound and so was her voice. The more anxious she became the higher her voice went.

We waited over an hour for Rob and Julio. By the time she concluded we had been stood up she was in full chihuahua register.

KAREN: : How dare they YIPE YIPE YIPE!!!

ME: Let's go back to the Alba. I'm tired.

KAREN: YIPE!- Can not believe this- YIPE YIPE!!!

ME: I need to go to bed. Do you mind if I go back?

She actually let me go! For the first time in almost a week she allowed me some alone time. I practically skipped back to our room; whereas little wholesome Karen slunk in around three a.m.

KAREN: (Stage whisper) Carrie. Carrie? (Full voice) CARRIE ARE YOU AWAKE?

ME: Am now.

KAREN: Guess what happened?

ME: You got drunk?

KAREN: No—ah! Maybe a bit tipsy, but Julio showed up!

ME: Why was he so late?

KAREN: He felt so bad!

ME: Did he have to wait until his wife was asleep?

KAREN: He apologized like crazy. Paid for everything! We had soooo much fun. What a dancer he is, and he taught me how to speak Mexican!!!

ME: That's nice. Can I go back to sleep now?

KAREN: Buenos nachos mon amigo!

After that night she spent every waking moment getting wined and dined by Señor Deep Pockets. I was finally free to enjoy my own company. I signed up for a few excursions, like horseback riding and parasailing. I played all the silly poolside games and even won a bottle of tequila for being the last person with an unpopped balloon on my ankle.

The two weeks of fun in the sun did me good. I stuck to my vow of celibacy. I weaned myself off the wiener and the

Robins Eggs. My heartrate had returned to normal. It was time to go home.

My travel partner didn't fare as well. On the day of our departure she burst into our room at five a.m. sobbing. She had just returned from visiting Julio... in jail. Turns out, Mr. Grande Spender was paying for everything with counterfeit cash. The police caught up with him and said they would let him go if she forked over enough pesos to cover what he had spent on her at the clubs all week.

ME: Tell me you didn't bail him out.
KAREN: His kids need their father.
ME: You bailed him out?
KAREN: I couldn't just let him rot in a Mexican prison! Who does that?!
ME: The cops were probably in on it!
KAREN: You are sooo cynical!
ME: You got scammed, Karen!
KAREN: You might act all mature but you still have a lot of growing up to do!

I didn't have much to say to her after that. It was a beautifully silent flight to Toronto until her three mini-bottles of chardonnay kicked in and she had to ruin it.

KAREN: I want you to know that was my first time...you know...?
ME: At an all inclusive?
KAREN: No—ah! I've been with my boyfriend since high school. We moved in together right after grad. Like I love him and everything but I think I'll probably find my own place, you know, for a while?

ME: Go get yourself some more hot beef injections of the international variety—Ole!
KAREN: YIPE! EW!! YIPE- YIPE- You are so gross- YIPE!!!

Maybe I shouldn't have been so flippant. She was ashamed of her behaviour and rightfully so. But seeking redemption from me was like confessing you got a speeding ticket to a Hell's Angel.

28

HOME ON THE ROAD

Dancers cluttered the booths of Lilly's Cafe, seeking comfort over a bowl of homemade mushroom soup or priming themselves with pre-shift shots of flaming sambuca.

Lilly befriended all of the dancers and she didn't mind if we loitered, as long as we ate our toast.

LILLY: You need something for the booze to stick to. Eat! Men don't like to hear da bones clanking. Eat, eat da toasts!!

I logged a lot of hours at the cafe. I ate the toasts and let Lilly mother me. She was always telling me I was special and I should go back to school, get a proper education, meet a nice man and have babies.

I assured her I had a plan (I didn't) and that I wasn't going to be dancing much longer.

It was so refreshing to have a grown up actually care about me. I would do anything for her.

LILLY: Tabida, I need from you a beeg favour. My brother Nicolie wants to lif da Canadian dream. To have good job, beeg house leef in pees. Understand? In order to become a citizen he needs to get a marriage. He's weeeling to pay $2,000 for a wife. She doesn't have to make de consumme wit heem. She must only marry and then she goes. What are you tinking of dis Tabida?

ME: I don't know. It sounds a little illegal or…

LILLY: Please Tabida, I ask only you because you are like da family to me. The daughter I always wanted.

ME: No consummee?

LILLY: shaking her head. NO of course not! But maybe you can make a nice dance for heem on stag night. I pay extra for dat.

I got married at the Niagara Falls City Hall to a 45-year-old man whose last name I can't pronounce. After the J.P. made us husband and wife we were ushered into an office to sign the marriage licence. The clerk behind the desk was a bald man built like a beer fridge. He was also a regular customer of mine from The Cabaret.

BALD MAN: Well well well. Congratulations Taba tha- aahhh. Carrie! Huh… You look nice dressed—I mean, in a dress. Hahaha! Clears his throat. We'll need you both to come back in a week to sign some final paperwork for Immigration Canada. In the meantime we'll do our background check on Mr. Kirshnuckgverovitch and pay our newlyweds a house visit. I look forward to your hospitality, Mrs. Kirshnuckgverovitch.

I slipped up and out through the AC vents and jumped head first into the falls.

LUKA: You vill have to come for deener. My wife she is a wheez in kitchen.

Luka gave me a grand as soon as we left City Hall. He promised the other half after the house visit. I kissed him on the cheek and said see you soon. Once he was out of sight I ran over to the travel agency. Georgina booked me a return flight to London, England. I paid in cash and this time she didn't offer to find me a travel buddy.

There were still months to kill before my European adventure but every fiber of my being was in flight mode—as in, get the fuck outta here—*now!* I didn't finish out the week at the Cab. I didn't say goodbye to Lilly and I certainly didn't tell my husband I was going back to Toronto on the next train.

It was obvious BALD MAN at City Hall knew I was a rental bride. It wouldn't take him long to learn I had two priors either. What was I thinking?! I was still on probation for fuck sake. I'd been threatened with the old, 'three strikes you're out!' enough times to be legitimately scared of being thrown in jail.

I hightailed it back home. I was looking forward to talking about Europe with Dad. He wanted me to travel and experience the world. He would be so proud that I actually booked a flight. He didn't need to know I purchased it with money from my new husband. I'd keep the conversation focused on what countries I should go to and all the museums I wanted to see. Dad would have a lot of opinions to share. Sadly, that conversation never happened. When I got to the apartment, Dad wasn't there. I was about to call Lesley to see if she knew his whereabouts but our phone was disconnected. I guess Dad hadn't paid the bill. Good. Luka wouldn't be able to reach me!

I didn't tell anyone I was married. I tried to put it out of mind. There was no way I could return for the house visit and to sign the final paperwork. In fact it was probably safest to avoid Niagara Falls all together. I could kiss the Cabaret goodbye and my home away from home, Lilly's Cafe. The hardest part of this whole ordeal was knowing I would never see Lilly again. Letting her down broke my heart. She trusted me to do this for the family and I royally screwed her over. That said, I like to believe she had no part in Luka's attempt at revenge.

It arrived in the mail about two weeks after our nuptials. While I couldn't understand the foreign language on the back, I certainly got the gist of it by the picture on the front. It was a black and white photo of a bludgeoned woman lying in an alley. The picture had been clipped from a True Crime magazine and then pasted on top of a Maid of the Mist postcard.

Luka was sending a message.

I got it loud and clear.

I had to get out of there. Luka knew where I lived! With Dad still MIA, I was terrified of being alone in our apartment. I booked a week of work at Fantashia's in Oshawa, hoping that by the time I got back Dad would have emerged from whatever bender he was on. The week in Oshawa went off without a hitch. It was a busy club which allowed me to take my mind off of the shitshow that was my life. I came back to Toronto a week later on a sunny Monday morning. From up the sidewalk I could see a piece of paper taped to our door. I quickened my pace. What the fuck? It was an eviction notice. My key didn't work in the lock. I stormed through the front door of the hardware store on the main level. The manager/owner/ landlord was behind the counter.

Let's call him Frank.

ME: Hey Frank. It's Carrie? I live with my dad upstairs.
FRANK: Yes. Yes, I know you.
ME: What is this paper all about?
FRANK: It's eviction notice.
ME: Yeah I can read, thanks. Why are you evicting us?
FRANK: You no pay rent, you no stay.
ME: I do pay rent. I pay rent every month to Dad!
FRANK: Dad no pay rent to me.

ME: What?!

FRANK: NO pay rent for months. I patient no more. No more patient!

ME: What am I supposed to do? What about all our shit?

FRANK: I let you in apartment. I give three days. You get three days. Then leave apartment. Take shit or leave shit here.

Now was not the time to get my own place. I was heading to Europe for two months. I needed somewhere short term. I took a bunch of quarters to the payphone across the street. Mom was the first person I called. She was still living with Dave. I hadn't been to his house since I stole the beans. But I was desperate enough to risk returning to the scene of my crime until Mom said, "I wish I could help sweetheart but I'm already overstaying my welcome here, you know, sorry. Try your Aunt Doreen. There's no one staying in their basement right now."

My aunt and uncle, who had done so much for me as a kid, didn't exactly receive me with open arms. They were reluctant to rent the suite to a stripper. I think they were worried I would corrupt their 15-year-old daughter. Regardless, their furnished basement suite was an affordable place to stash my stuff. And I truly loved my Aunt Doreen. Up until then she had always treated me like I was one of her own. I wanted to be close again. Maybe an edible peace offering would do the trick. I whipped up a crab-stuffed avocado and took it upstairs to her. I think she liked it. I'm not sure. She didn't say. She didn't say much at all. She was watching one of her shows. I sat there, watching her watch her shows. We said a few pleasantries before I slipped back into the basement ,grateful to have at least gotten Luka off my tail.

30

ESCAPE

I WAS PRETTY GOOD at keeping my vow to not sleep with the customers. But I've got a weakness for long hair, crooked smiles, and tight jeans. Who am I kidding? As long as they look remotely like a rock star I'm a smitten kitten. Scott checks all the bad-boy boxes. He even has a totally awesome tattoo of a deck of smokes rolled under the sleeve of a t-shirt, under the sleeve of his t-shirt. After my shift I do him on the seat of his '69 Triumph. The next day I move in with him and his parents. He's 29 and still lives at home. I ask Scott what's up with that.

SCOTT: 'Member that bike accident I told you about? No way I can work with my leg all gibbled up, man. See, look. He limps and winces. Besides, my folks are cool. Lotta people grow their own, but not everyone shares like they do. Fuck they know it helps with the pain too, right? What? Don't you like my folks? They meant what they said. They're gonna help you save your cash for Europe and shit. No charge for room and board all the free green you need. They're doing it outta the goodness of their hearts, man. They don't take in strays every day.

I don't tell him about Luka or the postcard. This stray knows when to keep her mouth shut. They offer up the couch in the living room. I am not allowed in their son's bed. They don't want no hanky panky under their roof. Soooo I play along, grateful to not be staying in the squalid strippers quarters above Fantashia's.

His Mom waits up for me each night and asks me to hand over my tips. She uncurls the pile of fives and puts them in her sock drawer. We hug and she tells me I done good. Me and Mom and Dad and Scott watch a lot of TV during the day. I realize while I'm watching that I'm not imagining myself inside the box anymore. I'm not daydreaming of being the chick in the red swimsuit jogging on the beach. I'm not dreaming at all. I'm too stoned or numb or sore or something and then Scott drops this:

SCOTT: My Workers' Comp came in. Thinking of checking out Europe with you, babe. Amsterdam, man. Me, you and some space cakes. Pretty fucking right on, eh?!

No fucking way. I don't want Scott tagging along. I mean, sure he's got a cool bike but Europe's about … about sitting beside an ancient … thing and writing … poetry. And finding myself and shit. Who am I? I mean, where the hell did I go? I'm 18-going-on-50 with no place of my own, a stalker, a grade 11 education. All I have is a plane ticket and a kick ass knapsack and I'm about to cash it all in. If I can't go to Europe alone I'm not going at all. It takes me two days to finally respond to Scott's sudden wanderlust.

ME: I don't know about Europe, man. Bad timing, right? I should probably stick around, get outta my aunt's basement. Like set up some digs, and for sure, like, go back to school. You know? Get my shit together. Hope you're not too disappointed?

SCOTT: Fuck no. It's not like I bought a ticket yet. Fuck Europe. It's got too many foreigners anyway.

Georgina the travel agent said I would need a doctor's note if I wanted a refund.

Scott's mom was on the phone in seconds. She had a hushed conversation with their family doctor. An hour later I went in to see her.

I had chronic bronchitis as a kid. It was easy for me to work up an angry cough. The doctor pretended to listen to my lungs and wrote me a note saying I had mono and was unfit to travel.

Great. Now I just had to bring the note to Georgina.

Scott was thrilled to have an excuse to ride to Niagara Falls. Me? Not so much but this had to be done. I hopped on the bitch seat and off we went. Pretty soon we're zipping past the neon of casinos, wax museums, Chinese food restaurants, seafood restaurants, Chinese seafood restaurants, and then SCOTT yells over the engine...

SCOTT: HEYYYY! I SAW A SIGN BACK THERE: HOMEMADE MUSHROOM SOUP. GONNA PULL A U-EEEY.
ME: (Lilly's Cafe?!?!?) NO!
SCOTT: OKAY OKAY I'LL PULL INTO THE GAS STATION, TURN AROUND IN THERE. TAKE A CHILL PILL.
ME: LET'S JUST GO TO THE TRAVEL AGENCY AND GET THE HELL OUTTA HERE!
SCOTT: I GOT THE SERIOUS MUNCHIES, BABE.
ME : SHUT UP! NOT YOU! THE THINGY. TURN OFF THE MOTOR, ENGINE NOISY THING! (He turns it off. The silence is more deafening than his muffler.) I need to tell you something. I did an illegal marriage thing here and this crazy Yugoslav–

SCOTT: You're married?

ME: Yeah. Well—No! I don't know. I never came back to sign the—

SCOTT: Jesus. You're married!?!? Why the fuck didn't you tell me?!

ME: I never slept with the guy. It was an arrangement. He didn't want a wife . He just wanted to be Canadian.

SCOTT: I don't believe this. Just when I was starting to… like you, you YOU'RE FUCKING MARRIED!

ME: I'm not! I don't think so. I DON'T KNOW! All I know is I can't stop for no GODDAMN MUSHROOM SOUP and I don't want to get arrested so let's just go to the travel agency and get this THE FUCK OVER WITH!

SCOTT: (Kicking over his beloved bike.) FUCK!!!

When I walked into the travel agency, I didn't fake an angry cough nor did I show her the doctor's note. "It was just a bad cold, Georgina!" No need for a refund. I bought my Eurail pass instead.

Scott didn't need to know this. I told him all had gone as planned.

ME: She fell for it. She even told me to gargle with saltwater and wear socks to bed.

SCOTT: Right on. About the other shit … don't ever fuckin lie to me again.

It was a long cold ride back to Oshawa. He dropped me off at work. I was grateful to be there, away from psycho boy. Little did I know that the real drama was about to begin.

I went into the changeroom and there in all her ghoulish glory was my old friend, Chantell.

CHANTELL: Hey sweetie long time no see.

We hug and she smells like Poison, both the perfume and the lethal stuff of medieval nightmares.

ME: Yeah really, eh, ha ha. No kidding.

CHANTELL: You're looking good girlfriend.

ME: Thanks. You too! I like your hair.

CHANTELL: I'm growing it out for my wedding.

ME: You're getting married?! Wow. Congratulations!

CHANTELL: October 31. All Hallow's Eve. Full moon and free acid for all the guests. Wanna come?

ME: Sure. Oh! Can't sorry. I'll be in Europe.

CHANTELL: That sucks. Come and do a stag with me tonight. Tiny, the bouncer's taking us. Five hundred each before tips. Be ready at nine.

I go out on the floor, do a few tables and keep my eye on the clock. At 8:55 I check for Chantell in the changeroom. She's passed out, face down in a mirror full of blow. I sneak out and tell Tiny, Chantell's not coming. I work the stag alone and pocket the grand. It's later than usual when I get back to Scott's. His Mom isn't waiting up for me. She thinks I've cancelled my trip. No need for her to guard my cash anymore. I sneak into their bedroom. My heart is beating so loud I'm afraid it will wake them. I open their sock drawer, reach in, grab my cash and slip back out. I'm on the next bus back to Toronto.

Okay okay okay. I got a ticket, a Eurail pass, passport, knapsack, a pocket full of cash! And just one week to kill before I fly the fuck outta here!!

The sun was starting to rise as I let myself into Aunt Doreen's basement.

There were no boogeymen waiting for me. Just an unmade bed that smelled of me only. I slipped under the covers and shut 'er down for a few hours.

I stayed busy during the days leading up to the trip by

packing and repacking the knapsack. I researched Europe at the library and got phone numbers of my German relatives from Oma. Dad had resurfaced too. He was full of remorse and still homeless, yet that didn't stop his attempts to educate me on which historical sites were must-sees.

Night shifts at The Pussycat Lounge were a breeze. I was so excited I bounced through the week effortlessly. It was less than 24 hours before take-off and I was working what I hoped would be my last ever shift as an exotic dancer. I was floating through the crowd with a big ass grin on my face, thinking, Nan-naa nan-aa boo boo. I'm so outta here. Tomorrow, all you clowns will still be hunched over your watered down draft and I'll be halfway around the world, drinking Guinness and eating exotic—

SCOTT: Hey babe. How's it goin?
ME: Wwwww Scott? Hey. Wow what are you–
SCOTT: You gotta big trip tomorrow, don't ya?
ME: I can explain. I- I- I- Sorry. I'm sorry. It's just I—
SCOTT: Sshhh. He puts a finger on my lips to silence me. The other hand reaches into his back pocket and produces an airline ticket. I'm coming with you!!!
ME: You gotta ticket?! HOLY FUCK! Totally awesome, babe. Let me grab my gear. I'll meet you 'round back.

This could not be happening. I would have peed my pants if I were wearing any. How the fuck did he find me? Shit. I had to move fast.

I got my bag and snuck out the front door where all the taxis were parked. I jump in the back seat, give the driver Aunt Doreen's address and duck my head low in the back seat.

ME: I need you to drive really really fast.

The driver is up for the challenge. We fly out of the parking lot. I hear a motorcycle closing in.

ME: We gotta ditch him.

TAXI DRIVER: Who?

ME: Do you see a guy on a bike?

TAXI DRIVER: A motorcycle?

ME: YES! PLEASE!!! LOSE HIM Go Go GO!!!!

TD: Is that a '69 Triumph?

ME: Yes! That's him! FUCK!!!

TD: Is he a bad man?

ME: Yes. Yes, very bad.

TD: Are you in trouble?

ME: Um. Only if he catches me.

The tires shriek as the driver does a sudden sharp turn.

I hear the motorcycle fade into the distance but don't pop my head up until the driver says

TD: We're here.

I exhale for the first time since Scott entered the Pussycat Lounge.

ME: Thank you thank you so much. That was some awesome driving.

I give him a fat tip.

TD: Thank you. Stay safe. Sleep well.

Sleep? Huh! I can't sleep. No freakin' way. How did he find me? Did he follow the bus out of Oshawa? Has he been watching me all week? Is he watching me now? I don't want to be watched anymore. I'm tired of being watched. I gotta get outta here. I'm getting on that plane. I don't give a shit if Scott or Luka or fuckin' Mitch is on it. I am getting on that flight. I paced and smoked until the sun came up. That's it. I'll go to the airport now. What the hell. Check in super early. Hide in the washroom. I'll be safe there. Lotsa people around. Yeah, safe. Good. Safe is good. Washroom clean, good, good and clean. Safe and good and clean. Call a cab. Call a cab. Now if I could just stop shaking…

I boarded the plane—alone. If Sean was on the flight I never saw him. I didn't run into him anywhere in Europe either. My best guess is the 'ticket' he produced from his back pocket was an empty envelope. He was just fucking with me. Regardless, it didn't take me long to stop looking over my shoulder and enjoy myself.

Ahhhh Europe. Everything's so rich and dense, like a good cheesecake. You have to really slow down to enjoy it. And I did. My days were spent going from museums to cafes to cafes to museums, filling up my belly and my notebooks. I let the German relatives spoil me and once in Amsterdam I wisely avoided the Red Light District. I fell in love with the Impressionists, smoked a cigarette in Westminster Abbey, and ate mussels in Brussels. My favourite place was Folegandros, a tiny Greek Island where donkeys are the only mode of transportation and everyone smiles. On one of my solitary walks, I met a man as old as the sun. He muttered something. I stopped. He reached into his pocket and held out a strange fruit. I reached into my pocket to offer him money. He shook his head and waved away my coins. Placing the fruit in my hand with both of his, his kind eyes told me everything was going to work out. He walked away, not wanting anything from me. I bit into the fresh fig. It tasted of earth and mystery and sex. Good clean sex. I ripped into it. The sticky juice dripped down my chin, and I didn't wipe it off.

Why bother? No one was watching.

THANKS

NOW, SOME THIRTY YEARS LATER, I am happily married (third time's a charm) with some brag-worthy career highlights but the most rewarding accomplishment by far has been raising my daughter.

Johanna Stickland lives the rich and deeply sensual life of an artist and I could not be more proud. Or relieved. I didn't fuck her up! In fact she's told me many times how grateful she is to have had such a magical childhood. Magical? Wow and Phew! Thank you, Johanna, for letting me bounce these sad and shocking stories off of you. You filled me with unabashed and much-needed praise. I owe you. Send me your therapist's bill!

Thank you, Rowan Hildebrand, my sexy dreamboat husband, for stoking the woodfire, cat sitting, and giving me space to write Thank you, Dad, for telling me that if I didn't write something someday it would be a goddamn waste of talent. I wish I'd kept you on the phone longer that day. Thank you, Mom, for always telling me I could do whatever I set my mind to. I miss you every day.

Thank you Eugene Stickland for encouraging me to write "The Bridge" — the story that inspired this book. Thank you, Lorene Shyba, of Durvile & UpRoute Books for believing in me and helping to make a dream come true. Thank you, Jennifer Theroux, (my soul sistah) and Meghan Whitsitt for your eagle-eye expertise proofreading wizardries. Thank you, Loretta Meyer, for capturing my inner badass and permitting us to use the image. I love this cover! Thank you, Jim Sheddon, for the last minute rescue of my old photos!

I need to thank other kind and supportive people who(m) I'm lucky to call friends; Tiffiny Aasen, Darla Biccum, Norm Bradshaw, T and A Brooks, Gaye Burgess, Richard Campbell, Shauna Chant, George Clairmont, Linda Cunningham, Vicki Dale, Georgélaine Dawn, Elena Evanoff, James Fulton, Anna Hart, Heather Hill, Heather Hodgson, Mark Kooting, Deidre Stoneburgh Lazar, Dini Middel, Paul Pitkanen, Andrea Prunty, Lori Ravensborg Schofield, Tc Sclocco, Kate Shane, Karen Shenfeld, Lorraine Thompson, Deb Tomlinson, Evie Walton, Lori Fleming Wilson, Penny Ward Wolfson, Joan Ververgaert, and countless others. I could not have gotten this done without you cheering me on from the sidelines.

What more could I ask for? Well there is one thing...

If my collection of memories inspires you to reflect on the stories that make you who you are today, take note. And should your trip down memory lane take you to the corner of Bad and Ass, please tell your stories! Share them with anyone and everyone. Don't wait for permission. Demand attention. You owe it to yourself and every little kid who cries themselves to sleep.

Thank you from the bottom of my very full heart.

— *Carrie Schiffler, 2022*

ABOUT CARRIE

Carrie Schiffler is an actor who writes and a writer who acts. Sometimes the two talents merge resulting in a one-woman show, most notably, Tabitha A Girl and Her Box, produced by Ground Zero Theatre in Calgary, Alberta. She also received an honourable mention for 'Lemon Opera' in Lorian Hemingway's short story contest 2016. Her first collection of poetry, Umbilicus is a meditation on the sensuous and includes images by her daughter, international artist Johanna Stickland. Calgary, Alberta and Burks Falls, Ontario both claim Carrie as a hometown treasure.